Connecting

WITH THE

Congregation

Rhetoric and the Art of Preaching

Lucy Lind Hogan
and
Robert Reid

ABINGDON PRESS / Nashville

CONNECTING WITH THE CONGREGATION
RHETORIC AND THE ART OF PREACHING

Copyright © 1999 by Abingdon Press

This book is printed on acid-free, elemental chlorine-free paper.

Library of Congress Cataloging-in-Publication Data

Hogan, Lucy Lind, 1951–
    Connecting with the congregation : rhetoric and the art of preaching / Lucy Lind Hogan and Robert Reid.
    p. cm.
    ISBN 0-687-08529-2 (alk. paper)
    1. Preaching. 2. Rhetoric—Religious aspects—Christianity.
    I. Reid, Robert, 1950–.II. Title.
    BV4211.2.H615 1999
248.4—d21   99-32837
                                                                     CIP

Scripture quotations are from the New Revised Standard Version Bible. Copyright © 1989 by the Division of Christian Education of the National Council of the Churches of Christ in the USA. Used by permission.

The excerpt on page 7 from Martin Luther King, Jr's sermon "The Drum Major Instinct" is reprinted by arrangement with The Heirs to the Estate of Martin Luther King, Jr., c/o Writers House, Inc. as agent for the proprietor.

Copyright 1968 by Martin Luther King, Jr., copyright renewed 1996 by The Estate of Martin Luther King, Jr.

99 00 01 02 03 04 05 06 07 08—10 9 8 7 6 5 4 3 2 1

MANUFACTURED IN THE UNITED STATES OF AMERICA

Connecting with the Congregation

Contents

Chapter 1

Who Needs Rhetoric?

PREACHING AS A RHETORICAL ART

On THE FOURTH of February, 1968 Martin Luther King, Jr. stood in the pulpit of Atlanta's Ebenezer Baptist Church. As his sermon on the tenth chapter of Mark was drawing to a close, Dr. King looked out at the congregation and pondered:

> If any of you are around when I have to meet my day, I don't want a long funeral. And if you get somebody to deliver the eulogy, tell them not to talk too long. Every now and then I wonder what I want them to say. Tell them not to mention that I have a Nobel Peace Prize, that isn't important. Tell them not to mention that I have three or four hundred other awards, that's not important. Tell him not to mention where I went to school. I'd like somebody to mention that day, that Martin Luther King, Jr., tried to give his life serving others. I'd like for somebody to say that day, that Martin Luther King, Jr., tried to love somebody.[1]

Dr. King was not speaking to a crowd of strangers. This was not a rally of civil rights workers. No, this was his congregation. While he and these people were engaged in a great struggle that would change the face of the United States, they were also engaged in the relationship between pastor and congregation. This was home. He was preaching God's Word to the people who knew and loved him. It was simply Dr. King, the one who baptized them, married them, and might one day bury them. Unfortunately, only two short months later, it would be this community that would bury Dr. King. When the time for the funeral

7

came, it was the congregation of Ebenezer Baptist Church that allowed Dr. King to speak his own epitaph by replaying these words from a tape recording of the sermon. They were words the congregation had remembered.

The wood of the pulpit in this church had been rubbed smooth, not only by Dr. King, but also by his father who had preceded him as pastor. Dr. King had been licensed to preach by Ebenezer Baptist Church in 1947, and, as pastor of the church, he preached there regularly between 1960 and 1968. He knew these people well. One need only listen to these words spoken shortly before his death to recognize his gifts as a speaker who employed *eloquence* in service to the gospel. For the people of Ebenezer, he regularly crafted messages with carefully chosen words and images served up, not on well worn, "everyday" dishes, but on the good, "company" china. It was this natural care and craft that made for such memorable messages.

In the prologue to his book *The Preacher King,* Richard Lischer lifts up the dynamic of King the preacher on the one hand, and King the architect of the Civil Rights movement on the other. He was "God's trombone and a doctor of philosophy in one and the same mission." The result was that, "Through a combination of personal gifts and historical circumstances, Martin Luther King, Jr., achieved the very thing that eludes us all today: *he framed a broadly based rationale for the equality, even the kinship of the races; and he advanced a method of attaining it.*[2] By careful attention to words and figures of speech, and by adaptation to his audience, Martin Luther King, Jr., found the pulpit to be what many have known and many have hoped it could be—a place from which to stand in order to move the world. Dr. King preached and the valleys began to be filled. Through his preaching the rough places were a little smoother, and the people of God were given an even greater glimpse of the reign of justice and freedom.

But what are we to make of the tension between doctorate and trombone? Are preachers the instruments upon which God plays in order to bring words of judgment or sweet melodies of comfort and release? Can preachers only pray and wait for the touch of the burning coal, the same coal that touched the lips of Isaiah? Or, are preachers trained up in the way? Are preachers born or are they made? Are preachers empty vessels waiting to be filled, or are they practitioners of an art or a craft?

This book gives a resounding yes to all of these questions. Yes, the mouths of preachers are touched with burning coals. Yes, human preachers can be, and are, the instruments of God's grace in the world. And yes, some people are truly *born* preachers. Years of preaching and teaching student preachers have convinced us that Paul was correct, preaching is a gift that some (not all) are given. Martin Luther King, Jr., was, indeed, a born preacher. But, we also wish to stress that yes, a preacher can be trained in the way, for there is an art to the craft of preaching.

While this question, whether preachers are born or made, has challenged the church since the earliest days, the authors of this book are firmly convinced that preaching is a skill that can be learned and improved upon, for preaching is a rhetorical art. That is, preaching is an art of connecting with the congregation. It is acquired through the knowledge of principles, through understanding how master preachers before us—such as King—effected their persuasive ends, and finally, through practice, practice, and more practice.

WHAT IS RHETORIC?

In *The Rhetorical Act,* Karlyn Kohrs Campbell defines rhetoric as, "The study of all the processes by which people influence each other through symbols, regardless of the intent of the source."[3] Rhetoric is the study of what is persuasive in human communication, whether intentional, or simply a consequence of the human condition. Rhetoric is concerned with all of the processes by which people use symbols to influence one another. And, as Kohrs Campbell also stresses, the issues with which rhetoric is concerned are social truths, addressed to others, justified by reasons, that reflect particular cultural values.[4]

What do we mean when we say that we use symbols to influence one another? We are used to thinking of water, bread, and wine as symbols because they are material, concrete entities that stand for or point to something else. But we forget that words are themselves symbols. For example, there is nothing intrinsic to the combination of sounds that comes out of the human mouth as *gras* (grace) that indicates God's favor and mercy toward the created world. Only by growing up within an English-speaking Jewish or Christian community will we come to have an understanding of this particular combination of phonemes.

Symbols, then, are something we learn. Water is a powerful symbol within the Christian community. The water of baptism is a symbol of new life, new birth. It reminds us of the flood, the parting of the Red Sea, the baptism of Jesus in the Jordan, the water used to wash the disciples' feet, and the water that flowed from the side of the crucified Jesus. But one does not automatically think of these connections when drawing a glass of water from the tap. We learn of the meaning of that symbol within the Christian community through a long process of worship, the reading of scripture, education, and the community's preaching. But even with these associations, we know that a farmer in Iowa, who has just survived another spring of flooding, will still react differently to the word *water* than will a Saharan farmer who longs for enough water for his or her crops. Symbols are grounded in a particular cultural community, and they change as the times change, depending on what will work for a community. Associations and even meanings for words like water, bread, and wine will necessarily be different for different communities. Undoubtedly, a Hindu will respond to the symbolic nature of water, or even the word grace, but that response will certainly not be the same as the Christian's response. Central, therefore, to the study of rhetoric as a symbolic activity is its *contextual nature*.

Ultimately, it is through the study of rhetoric that we come to learn to use the symbols of language to teach, to delight, and to move. Through symbolic actions we remind and reconnect people with their pasts, while urging them into creating new futures. We may expand a person's vision of the possible or turn another away from destructive behaviors.

Is it possible to see everything that we say or do as rhetorical?

This certainly is the view of some. Philosopher and rhetorician Kenneth Burke describes human beings as symbol-using animals. He says that we use symbols because we are animals who respond to the symbolic. Others argue that human beings can "never not communicate."[5] In all that we say and all that we do we are trying to make a place for ourselves in the world. Even through a look or a smile we are trying to *educate* the other, to *delight* the other, to *persuade* the other that we are trustworthy, thereby making him or her more receptive and willing to respond favorably to our wishes. We can "never not communicate." Everything we say to one another can be viewed rhetorically because, at a fundamental level, there is little we can say or do that does not have persuasive or influential implications.

However, when we speak of the *art* of rhetoric we quickly bring our focus to the analysis and production of specific rhetorical acts. In her work on rhetoric, Karlyn Kohrs Campbell makes a distinction between rhetoric and a rhetorical act. While she is willing to grant this very broad definition of rhetoric, that it includes everything we say and do, she also argues that there are instances which are an "intentional, created, polished attempt to overcome the obstacles in a given situation with a specific audience on a given issue to achieve a particular end."[6] According to this understanding, a persuasive speech or book, written for a particular group of people, at a particular time, in a particular place is an example of a rhetorical act.

Since antiquity, this phenomenon of producing specific rhetorical acts, or speeches, has been considered an art. By this, ancient philosophers and orators meant that certain theories and resources were available by means of which one was able to perfect the skill of communicating, or connecting, with one's audience.

PREACHING AS A RHETORICAL ACT

Another way to think about the relationship between rhetoric and a rhetorical act might be to recall the difference between *preaching* and a *sermon*. Preaching may be defined very broadly as the proclamation of the good news. Any time we hear people talking about what God has done for them, or when we see people doing good deeds for others, we may say that they are preaching. Christians preach through words spoken in love, through acts of kindness and mercy, and when advocating justice. But when we speak of a sermon, we think of it in the same way that Kohrs Campbell describes a specific rhetorical act. A particular preacher delivers a sermon to a particular congregation during a particular worship service. In this sense, the sermon functions as an "intentional, created, polished attempt to overcome the obstacles in a given situation."[7]

A Disputed Association

There has been some dispute about the relationship between rhetoric and homiletics off and on in the history of preaching. The dispute began almost from the outset of the Christian church and, in many ways, is still with us today. For example, one of the leading homileticians of the second half of the twentieth century recently posed the question of whether rhetoric should still have a place and a role in preaching. In an essay entitled, "Is There Still Room for Rhetoric?" Fred Craddock asks "whether or not the marriage between homiletics and rhetoric should be terminated."[8] While expressing grave reservations about the older model of rhetoric and the assumption that the preacher's task is to persuade, Craddock concludes that homileticians must revisit rhetoric with "a broader sense of its contributions," a conclusion that leads him to an unhesitating "yes!" in response to the question the title of his essay poses. Yet the question posed by his essay title tends to remain in the reader's mind more vividly than his purloined answer in the affirmative.[9]

Richard Lischer is equally concerned to articulate the relationship of a theologically grounded homiletics to the discipline of rhetoric. In a recent interview he affirmed the necessity of paying attention to rhetoric, but adds, "when we're talking about rhetoric I think it should be a rhetoric thoroughly informed by the Bible's theology and rhetoric rather than purely literary interests."[10] There is no simple division for Lischer, because the

"Gospel has its own rhetorical implications and these govern all other concerns."[11] The result of the latter is that preaching scripture often demands "[no]thing less than a rhetorical risk in the pulpit."[12] At the conclusion of the interview, Lischer returns to the subject of the relationship between rhetoric and preaching and acknowledges that this area represents one of the significant "gaps" in homiletical literature and that "a thorough analysis" is clearly needed.[13]

While, perhaps, coming at the question from different directions, both Craddock and Lischer do agree that there is a fundamental relationship between the art of preaching and the art of speaking (rhetoric). They also both agree that more work needs to be done to assist preachers in understanding the nature of this relationship, for if this relationship is ignored, or, even worse, rejected, it is the discipline of preaching that suffers.

As we begin to revisit the relationship between rhetoric and homiletics, we wish to state clearly that this book does not assume that a knowledge of the theory and practice of rhetoric is enough to make one an effective and energetic preacher. Preachers need to be both God's *scholars* as well as God's *trombones*. Learning rhetorical theory is not enough to make one an effective preacher. However, what follows is predicated upon the understanding that a knowledge of rhetorical theory can make one a more effective *trombone*. Effective preaching is effective rhetoric, and we cannot begin a theory of preaching pietistically devoid of an understanding of the art of rhetoric. It is only when the student and preacher understand the basics of the art of effective communication that they can explore how it is that theology affects this practice.

Recognizing Preaching's Rhetorical Dimensions

How then, can we shore up and rebuild this often shaky relationship between homiletics and rhetoric? What does it mean to view preaching as a rhetorical act? Perhaps we can see this by returning to our opening example. Few would argue that Martin Luther King, Jr.'s, life itself preached. He was, indeed, a persuasive *martyrion* (in the original sense of the term that stands

behind our word *martyr*), a witness to the good news in all that
he said and did. But if we think of his preaching according to the
definition of rhetorical act offered above, it becomes obvious that
there were times when Dr. King intentionally created and polished
a message to "overcome the obstacles in a given situation with a
specific audience on a given issue to achieve a particular end."[14]
Using what rhetorical theory refers to as tropes and figures of
speech, allusions to Bible passages, echoes of spirituals, stories,
and images, Dr. King shaped the symbols of language for a particular group of people.

If we look and listen closely to the brief excerpt with which we
opened this chapter, several aspects of the *rhetorical* dimensions
of King's words become evident:

- There is a sense in which we cannot avoid the assumption
that this kind of comment is called forth by the immediate
circumstances of King's life. Congregation and speaker alike
felt the power of these words, as do we afterward, precisely
because they are so prescient. From this text we can assume
that the audience was as aware as Dr. King that the threat on
his life hovered ever closer, making this kind of statement all
the more poignant. Rhetoricians describe this kind of statement as discourse *called forth* by the rhetorical situation.

- Even with these eight sentences we gather something of a
sense of King's application of style and rhythm used to
heighten the final assertions. Rhetoricians would note the
ease with which King uses the two schemes of repetition—
anaphora and *epistrophe*—to underline the significance of
the claims that come at the conclusion. *Epistrophe* is repetition of a word or phrase at the end of a clause (for example,
"that isn't important"). *Anaphora* is the repetition of the
same word or group of words at the beginning of successive
clauses (for example, "Tell them not to mention..." which
eventually becomes "I'd like someone to mention...").
These stylistic techniques of repetition are usually reserved
for situations in which the author wants to create a strong

emotional effect. Here we would say that King is using stylistic control in service of an appeal located in the *pathos* of the situation.

• More than any other group of people, we know that this congregation was already well aware of their pastor's credentials. They were equally aware of the reasons that the outside world might offer to authenticate his personal "value." A rhetorician would note that by reframing what really counts as *ethos*, King is seeking to shift the *ethos* appeal that others might make when trying to summarize the contribution of his life and character. It is obvious that he wanted it measured by gospel rather than credentials.

• If we ask why approach the subject in this way, the rhetorician would say that King is engaging in a form of topical reasoning, using one of the common topics (comparison) and one of its subtopics (difference). This kind of reasoning is especially relevant to categories of defense, where a person wants to put forward his or her side of a case. It uses contrast to arrive at understanding and to make an appeal by way of *logos*.

In offering this analysis we have looked at this excerpt from King's sermon through four different rhetorical lenses. The first lens examines the rhetorical situation, the way a text reveals the historical situation that made particular remarks appropriate responses. The remaining lenses are provided by the essential resources for understanding rhetorical proof, or what Aristotle called the *pisteis*. These are *pathos*—persuasive proof that arises as an effect of understanding who the audience is and the ability of the speaker to move that audience emotionally; *ethos*—persuasive proof that arises as an effect of the character of the speaker; and *logos*—persuasive proof that arises as an effect of the argument and rational linkages presented in the speech. Obviously there are some dimensions of this speech that homiletics is better suited to uncover (for example, its cadences as an indication of Black preaching style,[15] its implicit allusion to Paul's *apology* for his life in Philippians 3:4-9, the theological force of gospel as an *ethos* appeal), but it is significant that *rhetoric* and *rhetorical theory* provide the tools that actually help us to unpack the persuasive action of this text. This is because preaching is, by definition, a rhetorical act.

Of course, we are not suggesting that preachers need to become aware of the rhetorical dimensions of their craft so that they can put sermons together by the cookie-cutter method. We don't throw a little *anaphora* in with a common topic to arrive at a sermon strategy. The purpose of understanding the rhetorical dimensions of preaching is to be able to view the task rhetorically as well as theologically. So what would it mean theologically to view preaching as a rhetorical act? We would suggest that it begins with the following assumptions:

1. The Word of God is communicated to humans, mediated by, and in, language, culture, and history. The paradigm of this communication is the Incarnation. As Tom Long points out, "There is a scandalous fleshiness to preaching, and while sermons may be 'pure' theology all the way through Saturday night, on Sunday morning they are inescapably embodied and, thus, rhetorical."[16]
2. Preaching is expressed in language. When we use language we make choices, we select, we use symbols, we tell stories, we make arguments. We *compose* a sermon. It is constructed by a human being.
3. Preaching always occurs in a particular situation for a particular group of people at a particular time. Sermons are situated: "A rhetorical act creates a message whose shape and form, beginning and end, are stamped on it by one or more human authors with a goal for an audience."[17]
4. Preachers hope and intend that their messages will move and persuade people in the congregation. There is, therefore, a persuasive intent to preaching. This is true regardless of whether the preacher has a specific intention to persuade listeners or she is simply depicting a possible "world"—in which she invites her hearers to enter simply by listening—with her words.

5. To be responsible as well as ethical, preaching must strive for balance in its rhetorical stance.

THE VALUE OF A RHETORICAL STANCE AS THEOLOGICAL STANCE

In the mid-1960s, composition teacher Wayne Booth authored a panel paper for teachers of composition in which he called for a different way of thinking about the basic English composition course. The presentation has since become a classic in the field. He began by defining the problem of too many reasonable but unfocused papers he had received from students over the years and then concluded:

> The common ingredient that I find in all of writing that I admire ...
> I shall reluctantly call the rhetorical stance, a stance which depends on discovering and maintaining in any writing situation a proper balance among the three elements that are at work in any communicative effort: the available arguments about the subject itself, the interests and peculiarities of the audience, and the voice, the implied character, of the speaker. I should like to suggest that it is this balance, this rhetorical stance, difficult as it is to describe, that is our main goal as teachers of rhetoric.[18]

Booth was recovering the value of the classic "means of persuasion" for a new generation of teachers, and, in doing so, he reinforced the essential rhetorical balance that was implicit in the classic understanding that "they must be kept in *balance.*" Rhetoric becomes a dirty word whenever the means are isolated and become the writer's or, for that matter, the speaker's, end. For example, overemphasis on *logos* becomes a perversion of the persuasive task through overreliance on the subject (the *de facto* problem that Craddock identified in rationalistic homiletics) and results in what Booth labels the *pedant's stance.* Undervaluing the subject and overvaluing the pure effect of *pathos* becomes the *advertiser's stance.* Sacrificing substance and effect in order to convey personality, charm, or some other way of putting *ethos* forward becomes the *entertainer's stance.*[19] Booth argued that everything worth teaching about rhetoric could be summarized as helping students discover how to avoid these perversions by striking the necessary *balance* of the *rhetorical stance.*

We also see this as our task: to recover the value of the rhetorical stance for preachers and to help them formulate a constructive theology of preaching that takes seriously that preaching is, by definition, a rhetorical act. David Cunningham has recently challenged theologians to adopt this same stance as a means of "doing theology." In his book *Faithful Persuasion: In Aid of a Rhetoric of Christian Theology,* he argues that Christian theological discourse has shown an amazing tenacity in its efforts to cling to the presuppositions of Enlightenment rationalism.[20] He finds it amazing because the Enlightenment project was an effort to shift the process of how humans come to know and understand their world away from reasoning controlled by the concerns of faith toward reasoning controlled by rational evidences. Yet, far from clinging to rationalism's worldview, Cunningham willingly admits, and even embraces, the "radical contingency" of theological discourse by acknowledging that all Christian theology is reasoning conducted by means of persuasive argument. Once this is conceded, Cunningham finds, the viability of any analytic model for "doing theology" is seriously compromised.[21] In response, he presents a systematic apologetic for reformulating how theological inquiry can be conducted by reexamining rhetoric's three means of persuasion (ethos, pathos, and logos), and argues that theologians need to regard rhetoric as fundamental to what they do. "Rhetoric," he concludes, "can provide a worthy alternative to some of the most sacrosanct assumptions of modernity."[22] It is theology's commitment to the strategies of thought grounded in modernity that Cunningham wants to confront. He argues that rhetoric's rejection of what amounts to tautological certitude, its attention to concrete contexts and audiences, its linguistic sophistication, and its hermeneutical sensitivity grounded in *praxis*, all make it particularly relevant as an essential tool for "doing theology."[23]

If only to underscore the significance of Cunningham's challenge, we think it is fascinating that the rhetorician, Wayne Booth, has recently argued the obverse of this contention: that a serious study of rhetoric "finally requires a *theology* for its validation," that "the study of rhetoric does not lead only to a study of God-talk (alá Burke's *Rhetoric of Religion*), but it leads to a serious embrace of some conception, however loose-joined or 'plural-ized,' of the divine."[24] In asking the question "Rhetoric and Religion: Are They Essentially Wedded?" Booth responds with an emphatic "yes!" arguing that the future vitality of rhetorical study itself depends on the renewed vitality of a theology that comes to conceive its task rhetorically. He calls for a constructive theology that stops toying with needing to emulate modernity's rationalism or to hide its discourse in tiny enclaves within divinity schools. He asks for a theology that refuses to be embarrassed by the fact that its central claims are rhetorically established.[25] In this sense, Cunningham and Booth are both calling for theology and those engaged in theological discourse to adopt a rhetorical stance in their communicative task. The invitation, extended to all people who in their talk "do theology," is to make what is being called the "rhetorical turn."

WHY MAKE THE "RHETORICAL TURN"?

For preachers to become faithful partners in the ongoing con-versation between God and the church, homiletics must make this "rhetorical turn." This phrase, now used across the disciplines in the university, has become synonymous with the recognition that no body of inquiry can escape the fact that it conducts its talk and research by way of words and persuasion. Where Enlightenment rhetoric had been all but banished as little more than training in elocution by the end of the nineteenth century, the end of the twentieth century has witnessed the recovery of the vitality of this discipline as, once again, being at the center of philosophical thought. If we concede, with Heidegger, that "language is the house of being,"[26] we can understand why the "rhetorical turn" has swept across the human sciences. The broad interest in rhetoric throughout the modern university is now astounding.[27] In the introductory article to a volume of essays on *The Rhetorical Turn*, Herbert Simons writes:

This ideal of an emancipatory, dialogic rhetoric is one worthy of a central place in the academy. But it requires of us that we conceive of rhetoric, not simply as an art of proving opposites, but also as an art of arraying and comparing ideas after first having attempted to give each its most forceful expression. And it invites us to further conceive of rhetoric, not simply as an art of expression or of reader-reception, but as one of intellectual exchange . . . the conversation metaphor . . . implies as well that inasmuch as we are in this together, we had better attend carefully to how we converse and to who we are, both as speakers and as audiences.[28]

The rhetorical turn emphasizes the relational quality of inquiry as a means of seeking truth. The renewed interest in listeners, the renewed interest in the hermeneutics of understanding, the renewed interest in creating convictional understanding—all these are signs that homiletics has begun to make the rhetorical turn as well. But for preachers to make the rhetorical turn themselves, they need to have a fundamental theological understanding of a rhetorical stance in preaching.

The time has come for preachers to make the turn and begin to understand the essential relationship between homiletics and rhetoric. We think the metaphor of marriage used by Craddock, and for that matter Booth, to describe this relationship between homiletics and rhetoric ultimately leads to a misunderstanding about their related nature.[29] The marriage relationship is ulitmately one of separateness and difference. Men and women are different, and the marriage bond can be severed. Use of the metaphor suggests that the relationship between rhetoric and homiletics could be similarly severed? We say no. Of course, ways of reflecting on the relationship may become stale and lifeless, but to deny that preaching a sermon is a rhetorical act is to deny that preaching a sermon is a language act. Once a preacher stops thinking about the relationship between rhetoric and homiletics in terms of the marriage metaphor (with its allied images of "divorce" and "reconciliation"), he or she has begun the more profound task of making the rhetorical turn.

The assumption of this book is that preaching a sermon is, by definition, a rhetorical act. Preaching is, therefore, an art predicated on a set of skills that can be learned. The purpose of this book is to introduce students of preaching to the basic theory of the art of rhetoric as it applies to the task of preaching. We want to help preachers learn how to be intentional in thinking rhetorically about their homiletic task, to assist them in being able to adopt a rhetorical stance as part of a constructive theology of preaching.

WHERE ARE WE GOING?

In order to answer this question we need first to say where we are *not* going. There is a rich tradition in rhetorical studies of "handbooks" that have generally been a cross between the "how to" manual and a "dictionary of distinctions" with categories and subcategories within the art. Readers interested in distinctions between kinds of arguments, elements of style, or patterns of organization can readily find a variety of books that take up rhetorical dimensions of each of these subjects.[30] However, this is not where we are going, because this is neither a "how-to" manual of composition for preachers, nor is it a compendium of classificatory distinctions in the art of rhetoric.

Another place we are not going is to produce a "how-to" homiletic rooted in rhetoric. We are not dressing up Broadus's *On the Preparation and Delivery of Sermons* for a new generation.[31] We will consider the historical role of this famous rhetorical "take" on the task of preaching in the course of this study, but our work is not an effort to revisit its site.

Our purpose is simultaneously more theological and more theoretical than either of these kinds of approaches. Because we believe that preachers must understand the rhetorical dimensions of their theological task, because we believe that preachers must approach that task from a rhetorical stance, understanding that preaching is a rhetorical act, we want to offer an interpretation of the rhetorical tradition as it relates to the art of preaching. We are interested in introducing preachers to the ways rhetoric provides a perspective as well as necessary communicative resources for homiletic practice. We want to explore classical and contemporary applications of rhetorical theory in order to discover how these can function as homiletic resources and contribute to a constructive theology of preaching.

Where are we going? In the next chapter we try to provide a basic primer on the art of rhetoric as first discussed by people like Aristotle, Cicero, and Quintilian. We briefly trace the relationship of rhetoric and homiletics over the past two millennia with a goal of exploring the aspects of the theory of rhetoric relevant to the question of why a preacher would want to adopt a rhetorical stance in sermon making. By looking at the relationship between rhetoric and homiletics from the outset, we believe preachers will have a better understanding of how to think about the relationship today.

In chapter 3 we focus on the question of who listeners think the preacher is by what is wittingly or unwittingly communicated about the preacher's implied character in the sermon. We examine important concerns such as how a preacher can construct the authority of character and conviction in preaching.

In chapter 4 we focus on the question of how the preacher can help listeners come to care about what is being said. We examine the importance of making effective and appropriate use of the creation of identification and emotional appeals.

In chapter 5 we focus on the question of how reasoning functions in the sermon and how the preacher can figure out what he or she wants to say. We examine how ancient strategies of coming up with good reasons can still be relevant today.

In chapter 6 we focus on sermon form, and how controlling the strategy of a sermon helps the preacher to understand the way the sermon comes across for listeners. We examine how a preacher can learn to take control of the preaching intention implicit in the design of a sermon.

In chapter 7 we focus on the issue of style in considering what happens as people listen to the sermon. We examine how the way something is said is fundamentally related to the ways of knowing that can happen for listeners.

Chapters 2 through 7 include a set of questions for group discussion as well as suggestions for where you can read more about the ideas presented in each chapter. In part, our goal is to encourage homileticians and preachers to make the rhetorical turn. We think this happens when you, the reader, become a participant in the ongoing conversation. As communication theorists, we are convinced that learning increases exponentially when readers are able to take ideas they have encountered while reading and engage these same ideas in group discussion. So we hope you can find a group in which you are able to discuss the ideas and concepts of this book. If you are reading the book on your own, we encourage you to journal your way through the discussion sections. If you are using the book in a class or a workshop on preaching, we hope you find the questions helpful in stimulating group discussion. The "Continuing the Conversation" sections are intended to be suggestive, indicating the open-ended nature of the dialogue that can occur as we begin to think rhetorically and as we begin to adopt a rhetorical stance in our preaching.

In a final, brief chapter, we encourage you, the reader, to adopt this rhetorical stance in preaching. A "stance" is a posture you can adopt that becomes who you are and how you think through effective training and practice. More than a collection of techniques, we believe that learning and practicing an *art* is really about learning to look at the world in a different way. We believe that the preacher who adopts a rhetorical stance has taken the first step in developing the homiletic *art of preaching* in a manner that connects with the congregation.

READ MORE ABOUT IT

Wayne C. Booth. "The Rhetorical Stance," *College Composition and Communication* (October 1993); reprinted in *Landmark Essays on Rhetorical Invention in Writing*. Richard Young and Yameng Liu, eds. Davis, Calif.: Hermagoras Press, 1994.

Karlyn Kohrs Campbell. *The Rhetorical Act*. Belmont, Calif.: Wadsworth Publishing, 1996.

Fred Craddock. "Is There Still Room for Rhetoric?" In *Preaching on the Brink: The Future of Homiletics*. Martha J. Simmons, ed. Nashville: Abingdon Press, 1996.

Thomas Long. "And How Shall They Hear? The Listener in Contemporary Preaching." In *Listening to the Word: Studies in Honor of Fred B. Craddock*. Gail O'Day and Thomas G. Long, eds. Nashville: Abingdon Press, 1993.

Chapter 2

When Did All This Get Started?

It was a fateful day when the venerable John A. Broadus asserted, in the work that was to become the standard in its field for generations, that homiletics was a branch of rhetoric. American homiletics has not yet been completely reconstituted after this stroke which severed the head of preaching from theology and dropped it into the basket of rhetoric held by Aristotle.

    —David James Randolph, *The Renewal of Preaching* (1969)[1]

Designing a move [in a sermon] is not merely an exercise in rhetorical strategy. Obviously, preachers employ exegesis, theology, tradition, cultural analysis, and so forth in presenting ideas. Nevertheless, let us not disparage rhetoric. Rightly, rhetoric is concerned with shaping moves in such a way that moves will fit human consciousness, and there contend with the social attitudes that people bring to church. Ideally, people should *not* feel that they are being talked to so much as having conceptual meaning form in consciousness as their *own* thought process. So designing moves involves theological smarts and rhetorical skill— trained rhetorical skill.

    —David Buttrick, *Homiletic: Moves and Structures* (1989)[2]

THE NEED FOR CLARIFYING HISTORY

LISTENING FIRST TO Randolph and then to Buttrick, one should not find it surprising that there is a good deal of confusion concerning the role of rhetoric in preaching. Actually, a lot happened in the two decades between the time Randolph called for a "homiletic" free from ties to rhetoric and the time when Buttrick conceptualized his innovative preaching text, *Homiletic*, as a "basic

25

Christian rhetoric."[3] For his part, Randolph was understandably challenging a half-century-old conception that the primary task of a sermon was to offer convincing and impressive proofs for the truth of Christianity and its teachings. He chose to challenge the existing assumption that preaching strategy should be dependent on argument theory. According to Randolph, dependence on this preaching strategy over several generations had turned preachers into little more than second-rate lawyers, or what he called the Perry Masons of the pulpit who differ with their television counterpart only in that they *lose* all the time.[4] Randolph's challenge was so effective that twenty years later, Buttrick rightly felt the need to reclaim the significance of rhetoric's relationship to preaching. He purposefully cast his book as "a rhetoric" of Christian preaching and derived his key distinctions for preaching's "argument strategies" from the work of contemporary rhetoricians.[5]

Time and circumstance account for some of the disparity in these claims about rhetoric's role in preaching, but many preachers may wonder what all the fuss is about. Others come to the craft of preaching aware that there is what insiders might call "some history" in this relationship. Yet all they know is the most recent squabble. Understandably, preachers wonder, "When did all this get started?"

We respond by saying that neither the history nor the debate is new. In fact, we see it as part of an ongoing conversation that has been happening across the centuries. To understand why the conversation has occasionally become volatile necessitates a basic introduction to ancient rhetoric, to ancient homiletics, and a brief account of the vicissitudes of this dialogue. The guiding maxim of this chapter is a familiar refrain: to discover where we are, we first have to know from whence we have come.

"JUST SO MUCH RHETORIC": THE ANCIENT ART OF CIVIC INVOLVEMENT

By almost any criteria, rhetoric's name has been mud for much of the twentieth century. In popular usage it has become a word used to disparage someone else's arguments: "My opponent's speech on the environment was just so much rhetoric!" "The candidate gave us nothing but rhetoric when what we need is solutions." People generally use the word to suggest that someone else's talk is merely an attempt to "spin" or manipulate the facts. Of course the irony is, that in matters of dispute, everyone's talk is "just so much rhetoric." In its most classical form, rhetoric has always been an exercise in the art of persuasion relevant to matters open to dispute. As an academic discipline, it is a means of inquiry concerning principles that, once mastered, permit more effective communication by people using language to accomplish their purpose. For more than two millennia we have used rhetorical principles as a means to come up with ideas about what to say, how to reason about it, and how to persuade others to accept our conclusions.

Consider the apostle Paul. At one point he states, "I may be untrained in speech, but not in knowledge" (2 Cor. 11:6). At face value it sounds as if he is confessing to a lack of education in the rules of rhetoric. Yet, as an educated Roman citizen, we can assume he was quite familiar with the rhetorical theory of his day because it was the basis of all secondary education in the first century B.C. Actually, the noun in this passage, *idiotes*, does not mean "unschooled." Paul is merely stating that, just because he is not a professional speaker, the Corinthian Christians should not assume that he is also unschooled in reasoning or that he lacks knowledge. This is a very *plausible* counterargument, directed to the experience of his audience as to why his authority should not be discounted simply because orators more eloquent than he had arrived on the scene. For all his protestations, Paul acquits himself as an extremely capable student of Greco-Roman argument theory in the wide variety of epistolary genres (from circumstantial *protreptic* and *apotreptic* in 1 Corinthians to *diatribe* in Romans).[6] His skill in these venues makes sense when we realize that teenage students in antiquity were literally drilled on ways to make "plausible" arguments and techniques to "embroider and stylize" phrases if the occasion called for it. Principles of theory and practice could be found in such works as Aristotle's *Art of Rhetoric,* but students were more familiar with the wide variety of technical handbooks that served as compendiums, naming and defining every option that might be advantageous to a speaker. Even the great Roman orator and politician Cicero began his public career by producing one of these handbooks (ca. 80 B.C.). He says that it was meant to be a synthesis of what others before him had said on the subject of how to make an argument.

By the second half of the first century A.D., during the same period most of the literature of the New Testament was composed, the Roman rhetorician Quintilian produced what would become the first truly comprehensive discussion of rhetorical theory in antiquity. From A.D. 71 to 91 he held a government funded Professorate of Rhetoric in the capital city of the empire and in A.D. 93 he published his accumulated lectures in a twelve volume work titled *On the Education of the Orator*. It was one of the first great surveys and historical synthesis of a discipline ever published. With good cause, too. By the first century A.D., practical understanding and training in the art of oratory was considered the preeminent preparation for entry into all aspects of civic life. Handbooks on the subject were ubiquitous. During the period in which crosscultural preaching lifted Christianity out of Judean obscurity, the course in rhetoric was considered the basic primer in effective communication for citizens of the Roman Empire.

Taken together, the rhetorical writings of Aristotle, Cicero, and Quintilian make for an excellent introduction to this ancient art of civic involvement. A modern professor of communication theory would describe this same education as an introduction to the art of critical thinking skills. So, to understand the foundation of this art we begin with these three ancient rhetoricians whom we will refer to at different points throughout this book.

Aristotle on the Art of Persuading as Civic Discourse

By definition rhetoric was conceived as an art of reasoning in probable matters relevant for persuading audiences, an art of making plausible arguments intended to win over audiences on topics where issues of "truth" are not at stake. According to Aristotle it was one of three kinds of argument, or ways of reasoning. As the art of plausible argument, he found that *rhetorical argument* is different from *logical argument*, which tries to emulate the certainty of mathematics in its quest for "valid" truth. He also found *rhetorical argument* is different from *dialectical argument*, which uses arguments that are probably "valid" to reason its way toward truths educated people would be willing to accept. *Rhetorical argument* is different from these other two. What really matters in rhetoric is not truth, but whether arguments appear reasonable to the crowds.[7]

Truth and validity are not at stake if your purpose is to persuade people to render a verdict, enact a policy, or reflect on a value. According to Aristotle the goal of this kind of civic reasoning is to influence people to judge fairly, to act expediently, or to respond honorably. This is why rhetoric is an audience-centered rather than a validity-centered form of reasoning. As the art of *persuasion*, it helps speakers focus on what makes for plausible arguments. The problem of figuring out the difference between what listeners will accept as plausible or convincing arguments, and what will come off as implausible or specious arguments, captures rather well the problem that rhetoric has always faced. Done well it will stir the hearts and minds of listeners. Done poorly it evokes contempt and hostility.

With this in mind, consider Aristotle's definition of rhetoric: "Let rhetoric be defined as an ability, in each particular case, to see the available means of persuasion."[8] In other words, it is primarily an ability concerned with *means of persuasion*. Its function as a *means of reasoning* is a secondary capacity of skill that arises from the "seeing."[9] A modern rhetorician has contemporized the definition in this way: "Rhetoric is the art of finding and employing the most effective means of persuasion on any subject, considered independently of intellectual mastery of that subject."[10] In either version, notice that the operative phrase is "means of persuasion." At first look, we might readily conclude that rhetoric is persuasion by *any* means "available." This is not so. Aristotle follows this definition by limiting the search for the *means of persuasion* to three factors:

ethos, which is persuasive plausibility that arises as an effect of the persona or character projected by the speaker—who listeners think we are;

pathos, which is persuasive plausibility that arises as an effect of understanding the audience and the ability to move them emotionally—why listeners should care; and

logos, which is persuasive plausibility that arises as an effect of using what are perceived as *good* reasons—what we are going to say to listeners.[11]

In other words, Aristotle knew that good speakers must consider the plausibility of what they will say, which makes the task of considering the persuasive effect of *pathos* and *ethos* every bit as relevant as the quality of the actual arguments *(logos)*.

Cicero and Quintilian on Artfulness in Persuading Audiences

After Aristotle, Cicero is considered the most important rhetorician in antiquity. He was more concerned with the practice of oratory than the theory of rhetoric and is most famous for commending that good speakers have a duty to make a synergy of three purposes in any given moment during a speech. Speakers must be able to move an audience, teach them, and please them. And where Aristotle argued for a moderate *mean* in all matters of style, Cicero was famous for calling on speakers to be well versed in varying style (whether plain, temperate, or grand) to the needs of the moment. In one of his mature dialogues, *On Oratory*, he has a character affirm the centrality of Aristotle's three *means of persuasion* by arguing that success in oratory arises from "the proof of our allegations, the winning of our hearer's favour, and the rousing of their feelings to whatever the case may require."[12] But notice how Cicero's way of presenting these ideas gives more presence to the sense of stylistic force as a factor of persuasive speech. With Cicero, the best orator is not simply one who is able to combine the three forms of rhetorical proof to effect the best argument. The best orator is also one who knows how to move, teach, and please an audience while doing it.

Quintilian's definition was purposefully less complex than that of Aristotle. He defined oratory in a way that was later turned into a simple Latin dictum: *vir bonus dicendi peritus*—"the good man speaking well."[13] He found Aristotle's definition of rhetoric too narrow precisely because it privileged the rational process of coming up with credible arguments (the process of "invention") almost to the exclusion of the use of good form in its expression. Even more than Cicero before him, Quintilian championed the idea that learning how to "speak well" required as much attention to the persuasive force of style and arrangement as knowing how to make *plausible* arguments. For Quintilian, definitions of rhetoric that are limited to the three means are invention heavy. For example, he says, "without style it cannot possibly constitute oratory."[14] Aristotle's discussion of rhetoric had placed more emphasis on *logos* and coming up with plausible arguments than on *ethos* or *pathos*. Like many of his philosophical contemporaries, Aristotle was attempting to domesticate some of the more unruly civic practice of democracy. However, by the time Quintilian was writing, Greek democracy was nothing more than a failed policy of a utopian past. Hence, his definition reflects more regard for an orator's ability to achieve an appropriate force of expression.

The Art of Rhetoric Across the Centuries

Two centuries after Aristotle and a generation before Cicero, a philosopher tried to dismiss the significance of matters of style and arrangement with the Stoic-like dictum, *"tene rem, verba sequentur"* which means "deal with your subject; the words will fall into place." Although Aristotle might have been sympathetic to the Stoic wish to *restrain* combative appeals, he still would not have approved the central role this advice would come to have in the rhetorical debate over the value of style and arrangement in the first centuries B.C. and A.D. No matter how much he preferred argument and proofs, he acknowledged that style and arrangement served important functions. The debate became somewhat academic after Cicero when the Roman political climate changed from a republic to an absolute monarchy. During this period the place of public debate and the use of speeches as political expression dramatically diminished. Imperial power abolished counsels in which public policy had formerly proved to be amenable to the power of persuasion. What once were public forums became venues for little more than performance declamation and the ramblings of philosophers.

By the fifth century A.D. rhetoric had been reduced to being merely the fifth of seven liberal arts. However, for much of the last two thousand years the rhetorical treatises of Aristotle, Cicero, and Quintilian have served as the central texts for the study of civility in public discourse. They also served as the basis of homiletical education in the church as well. Across two millennia, rhetoric's art has contributed to the growth and development of cultures and knowledge. For example, most students of American history know that the nineteenth century was considered the "golden era" of political oratory. The enduring homiletic effect of this Ciceronian ability to use the plain, temperate, and grand styles to variously, teach, please, and move an audience was still readily apparent in the preaching ministries of Harry Emerson Fosdick and Martin Luther King, Jr. By the beginning of the twentieth century, what had become the genteel rhetoric of eloquence had too easily conflated the use of refined words with refined morals. It was already giving way to a new and different kind of rhetoric—the carefully reasoned plain style of "the disciplinary expert."[15] But from a rhetorical point of view this is merely a shifting of emphasis among the means: pathos stock went down in favor of ethos. It still was, and is, all rhetoric.

How important has the study of rhetoric been during the last two millennia? In his role as an Oxford Don of English literature, C. S. Lewis observed that our lack of understanding the significance of rhetorical theory in previous centuries is the single "greatest barrier between us and our ancestors."[16] We think this is equally true when it comes to understanding the nature of our own homiletical inheritance.

ORATORY AND PREACHING:
PLAUSIBLE ARGUMENT MEETS GOSPEL
PROCLAMATION

Many words serve to describe the facets of preaching in the New Testament—proclaiming *(keryssein)*, announcing good news *(euangelizesthai)*, conversing *(homilien)*, witnessing *(martyrein)*, teaching *(didaskein)*, prophesying *(propheteuein)*, and exhorting *(parakalein)*. No one word embodies all that preaching became in the generations after the first century A.D., but the original ministry clearly had its roots in Jewish synagogue preaching. Jewish preaching, like that engaged in by Jesus and Paul, was a discourse offered in the synagogue (cf. Luke 4:14-30; Acts 13:16-41). This origin in Jewish worship began with a reading of a pre-established text from the Torah or from the Prophets and was followed by an interpretive lecture offered by a rabbi or an invited guest who applied the interpretation to the life of the congregation.[17] This influence is formative, but we must remember that much of the New Testament and early Christian preaching was offered to non-Jewish audiences. Greco-Roman audiences would understandably expect public speeches to conform to the principles of appropriate civic discourse in the Empire, otherwise the message, regardless of how vital, would fall on deaf ears.

During the next four centuries of the Christian era what became known as the "homily" was viewed primarily as a talk or a formal conversation that had as its goal the interpretation and application of gospel for either the converted or the unconverted. In other words, the nature of the audience determined whether the presentation was didactic or evangelistic. The preacher, in turn, determined whether the purpose was doctrinal, expository, or hortatory. Scripture was employed primarily in quotation or application rather than as a "text." Except in exposition, our modern notion of using scripture as a text for preaching is just that—a modern notion. The structure of a homily was idiosyncratic and usually short. For example, the preacher of the fourth or fifth century was likely to offer either an unstylized verse by verse exposition of scripture or an hortatorical homily filled with *paranesis, exhortio* and *exempla*. Much of this preaching was rooted in the rhetoric of catechesis, of explaining the meaning and implications of gospel to an audience already willing to accept the *truth* of the matter. And it was this commitment to the *truth* of scripture as God's holy word that was behind the early church's rejection of the formal art of rhetoric in preaching.

Augustine and the Problem of Truth

Early Christian leaders decided they wanted no part of rhetoric. They generally held all secular philosophies and disciplines in low regard, but their rejection of rhetoric was often singularly vehement. In part, their distrust may be traced to the emphasis upon using stylistic contrivance and sophisticated ornamentation which characterized rhetoric of this period. Basil of Caesarea decried the use of rhetoric as consumed with issues of eloquence in speech. Christian preachers, he charged, should seek a simple clarity of expression rather than obeying the "laws of encomium and other sophistic vanities."[18] He was not alone in his rejection. Jerome narrates a dream in which he stood accused by God of not truly being a Christian: "Thou art not a Christian, but a Ciceronian. Where thy treasure is, there is thy heart also."[19] Church leaders were virtually monolithic in their rejection of rhetoric. The passion with which rhetoric was singled out and disavowed may be a reflection, in part, of the number of church leaders who were turning their back on their previous profession as teachers of rhetoric,[20] but it was also a reflection of the fact that Christian leaders believed that preaching *truth* and making *plausible arguments* were incompatible tasks. Because they accepted the Bible as divinely revealed, they saw no need to make use of an art of plausible argument. Functionally, they treated preaching as a form of demonstration, the kind of proof derived from formal logic. Christian scripture was treated as the final, authoritative *truth,* and it was the Spirit that bore witness to the *truth* of God's word, not the opinion of persuaded audience members. For this reason, the early church leaders concluded that adding the artifice of persuasive techniques would only obfuscate the *truth* and deny the work of the Spirit.

This was the polarized situation between rhetoric and preaching that Augustine faced in his effort to reclaim the value of rhetorical principles for preaching in *On Christian Doctrine*, the first theoretical treatise on homiletic theory. Augustine, having been a teacher of rhetoric before he became a Christian, observed that the public orators were engaging and entertaining, while preachers of the truth were "sluggish, and frigid, and somnolent"(4.2). In other words, preachers were boring and were putting people to sleep. To remedy the situation Augustine realized that he needed to draw on some of the tools of his former profession. In *On Christian Doctrine*, Augustine conceded that, "There are also certain rules for a more copious kind of argument, which is called *eloquence*, and these rules are not the less true that they can be used for persuading men of what is false; but as they can be used to enforce the truth as well, it is not the faculty itself that is to be blamed."[21] He maintained that preachers could still benefit from the "human institutions such as are adapted to that intercourse with men which is indispensable in this life—[these] we must take and turn to a Christian use." And more than simply using rhetoric to make argument for truth, Augustine even called for a measure of Ciceronian eloquence, "He, then, shall be eloquent, who can say little things in a subdued style, moderate things in a temperate style, in order to give pleasure, and great things in a majestic style, in order to sway the mind."[22]

In effect, Augustine carefully tears down the artificial wall which his predecessors had constructed between the sacred and the secular tasks of persuading people through discourse. His reintroduction of rhetoric into the business of preaching is carefully guided and guarded. He does not prescribe a form for the homily. He offers no list of commonplace topics (a subject we will discuss in chapter 5), lines of argument, or themes, and his discussion of how to determine what to say (rhetorical invention) is really an introduction to the art of biblical hermeneutics. Throughout *On Christian Doctrine* he carefully defines his purpose as that of developing principles for ascertaining the proper meaning of scripture (the first three books) and the proper mode of making known that which is ascertained (the fourth book). He justified this introduction of the art of rhetoric into the vocation of the Christian teacher and preacher by questioning who would "dare to say that truth in the person of its defenders is to take its stand unarmed against falsehood?" (4.2). To the tradition of the homily, Augustine added significant elements of the art of persuasion with a clear eye directed to confronting the false teaching of heretics and schismatics.

The Growing Interdependence

From the time of Augustine throughout the Middle Ages, the task of preaching and the art of rhetoric circled each other, with the former drawing more and more from the latter, but always with cautious caveats about the dangers of a full embrace. For example, during the eleventh century the sermon was still practiced as a kind of inorganic homily with no formal introduction or divisions. Things began to change as the notion of preaching themes emerged in eleventh century Europe.

One homiletician proposed four ways for preachers to interpret a scripture text:

> The first is history, which speaks of the actual events as they occurred; the second is allegory, in which one thing stands for something else; the third is tropology, or moral instruction, which treats of the ordering and arranging of one's life; and the last is ascetics, or spiritual enlightenment, through which we who are about to treat of lofty and heavenly topics are led to a higher way of life.[23]

After this period, scripture was increasingly examined not as text, but *for* texts which the preacher might thematically amplify. This is true in Alain de Lille's *On the Preacher's Art* (ca. 1199) which is also the first homiletic textbook composed as a *rhetoric of preaching*. The thirteenth century witnessed an explosion of formal rhetorics of preaching. More than three hundred individual treatises on this subject still survive from this period. Whatever fears the Christian leaders may once have held about such a secular art, as Christendom became increasingly synonymous with the resident culture, the fears appear to have faded in proportion with the diminishment of secularity itself.

Discussions of homiletics were increasingly organized by the model of the taxonomic approach of the ancient rhetorical handbook tradition, filled with definitions and lists of options. And far from *truth* needing no assistance from the humanistic art of persuasion, the practice of preaching had become the means by which a preacher "persuade[s] the multitude, within moderate length of time, to worthy conduct." Robert of Basevorn, the author of this definition, not only details numerous commonplaces or themes appropriate for this kind of preaching in his fourteenth-century *Form of Preaching* (ca. 1322), but he also describes an extensive structure for a "three point" sermon which develops a theme, "because a threefold cord is not easily broken."[24]

Although the late-medieval preacher used this form of sermon to organize tropological expositions of scripture for moral purposes, the shift from an inorganic, unstructured narrative to a tightly reasoned argument, developed and amplified with considered care, provided the rationalists of the Renaissance with a sermon form highly suited to the doctrinal program of the Reformation. The moralistic sermon was certainly not abandoned, but even for Aquinas the literal sense of the passage was affirmed as the primary sense upon which any of the three spiritual senses must rely.[25]

By the time of William Tyndale in 1528, the tropological approach to preaching was being vilified as a simplistic alternative to challenging audiences with the "plain meaning" of scripture. In part, this sounds like the old denouncement of rhetorical eloquence in sermons by Basil of Caesarea. But unlike Basil, this English reformer had no quarrel with arguing persuasive points in a sermon. Tyndale may have been deeply frustrated with the simple moralism of thematic preaching in his day, but he expressed no frustration with the emerging form of sermon organization originally devised to present tropological interpretations of scripture. In fact, like so many other reformers, this sermon form admirably suited his purpose in making argument against the Pope and what he viewed to be the papal control of scriptural interpretation. In many ways, preaching had become synonymous with argument and with which confessional tradition offered the *most* reasonable interpretation of scripture, *most* reasonable practice in the church, and *most* reasonable understanding of the Christian life. The Reformation sermon form entered the modern era undergoing modifications over time for purposes of clarity of reasoning and audience patience rather than objections to its Enlightenment presuppositions, but it became in this era argument in the *most* classical sense.

Puritan preaching came to embody this conception of the sermon *as* rational argument. Most preachers can readily see the relationship between viewing the sermon as argument and Reformation politics, but as the rhetorician Michael Halloran observes, "It would be difficult to make sense of a Puritan sermon except as a deliberate application of Ramistic rhetoric."[26] In other words, it is as much a product of Enlightenment rationalism as it is Protestant *Puritanism*. A typical Puritan sermon was organized quite formally with the following divisions: (1) "opening" by reading a biblical *text;* (2) explaining the historical circumstances of the *text;* (3) defining key words and or unclear reference; (4) thematically developing the doctrines arising in the *text* or doctrines logically deducible from it; (5) supporting the arguments in the doctrine section with "reasons," especially by way of scripture citation; and, finally, (6) applying the sermon in a section variously called "uses" or "improvements" in which the preacher brought the doctrine to bear on practical living.[27] One needs only look to popularly anthologized versions of Jonathan Edwards's famous "Sinners in the Hands of an Angry God" to see how closely he adheres to this theory of sermon arrangement.

In the Yale lectures on preaching in 1877, Phillips Brooks noted that the preaching of *texts* had characterized Christianity for the better part of six hundred years. Even "a page of the Bible torn out at random and blown into some savage island seemed to have in it the power of salvation."[28] Brooks argued that the prevailing notion was that each verse was clothed with an independent sacredness of meaning. Texts supported themes for preaching and doctrines for theology. Even today, we occasionally hear a call to return to preaching "the great themes of the Bible," as if this represents an ancient and, therefore, more biblical homiletics. But this notion of thematic preaching carries with it assumptions about sermon form and sermon purpose that are much more recent. And even more recent is the assumption that sermons should present an argument to prove the *truth* of one particular biblical interpretation as the *right* interpretation. This kind of preaching owes its heritage to a complex interplay between Enlightenment rationalism and the Protestant Reformation.

The Sermon as Argument: Two Nineteenth-Century Trajectories

As we have presented the picture, homiletic theory had become increasingly dependent on argument theory, rules of evidence, and "proving" the truth of a particular way of interpreting gospel. By mid–nineteenth century, rhetoricians like Oxford's Archbishop Richard Whately viewed rhetoric as a branch of logic and designed his rhetoric to assist preachers and Christian apologists who were refuting scoffers by providing a theory of argument in support of the validity of revealed truth. In Whately's *Elements of Rhetoric* the great ideas of the Enlightenment concerning empiricism, rationalism, and psychology had all found a secure place within the rhetorical tradition.[29] Two great homileticians of the nineteenth century were thoroughly schooled in Whately's rhetoric. They were the Catholic apologist and theologian John Henry Newman, and the Baptist seminary professor John Broadus. The former saved Catholic preaching from this version of rhetoric, while the latter fully embraced it.

Newman was not only a student of Whately at Oxford, he was also a man whose mentor once admitted that if he were given three wishes, they all would have been for a mind like Newman's.[30] Newman's *rhetorical theory* is carefully detailed in a classic work of rhetorical apologetics, *An Essay in Aid of a Grammar of Assent*, and in his *Oxford University Sermons*. He wisely foresaw the problems with the way Whately located assent to belief in Enlightenment reasoning, countering that "Logic makes but a sorry rhetoric with the multitude. . . . Logicians are more set upon concluding rightly, than on right conclusions"[31] and that "deductions have no power of reason."[32] He saw faith as something which "science cannot determine" because final assent to faith can only be arrived at as the conclusion of rhetoric's "converging probabilities," not logic's "proofs."[33] Though he was charged with "irrationalism" following publication of the *Essay*, by the middle of the twentieth century religious leaders across confessional traditions had come to realize that Newman penned the primer for theological reasoning and reflection for a century in which rationalism had finally come to be suspect.[34]

If Newman shepherded Catholic homiletics away from a full embrace of Enlightenment rationalism, Broadus led Protestant preaching well into its fold. First published in 1870 Broadus's *On the Preparation and Delivery of Sermons* went through numerous revisions and was used extensively until the late 1950s. He defined homiletics as "a branch of rhetoric, or a kindred art," arguing that preachers should "regard homiletics as rhetoric applied to this particular kind of speaking." In the "Author's Preface" he stated,

> The subject of Argument is thought by some to be out of place in a treatise on Homiletics or on Rhetoric in general. But preaching and all public speaking ought largely to be composed of argument, for even the most ignorant people constantly practice it themselves, and always feel its force when properly presented; and yet in many pulpits the place of argument is mainly filled by mere assertion and exhortation, and the arguments employed are often carelessly stated, or even gravely erroneous. Treatises on Logic teach the critical inspection, rather than the construction of argument, and so the latter must be discussed in works on Rhetoric, if anywhere. The well-known chapters of Whately have been here freely employed [in this book], but with very large additions, and with the attempt to correct some important errors. The examples of argument given are nearly all drawn from religious truth.[35]

Broadus was so thoroughly committed to the rationalist rhetoric of Whately that many twentieth-century homileticians unfairly place the blame for the "rationalist turn" in homiletics on Broadus himself. But this overlooks the fact that the most influential works of rhetorical theory in the late-eighteenth and first half of the nineteenth centuries, whether those of Whately, Blair, or Campbell, were all written by Protestant clergy and all contained significant sections on use of argument in sermons and pulpit eloquence.[36]

In defense of Broadus, his book represented a significant effort to recover a more classical theory of argument for preaching. It differs from those of his predecessors by returning to the single subject of homiletics rather than presenting it as a subsection of rhetoric in the manner of British university rhetorics. David Buttrick has noted that whatever faults we might attribute to the work, it was a substantial, thoroughly informed rhetoric of homiletics, as opposed to the abbreviated "how to" handbooks on homiletics published in the central decades of the twentieth century.[37]

CONTEMPORARY REACTIONS
AND THE SEARCH FOR BALANCE

Our brief summary of the history of homiletics and rhetoric should make obvious that any discussion of preaching *theory* must come to terms with the way in which successive generations over the last two millennia have witnessed what Broadus called "the kindred relationship" between rhetoric and homiletics. In the three decades since Randolph originally rejected the influence of rationalistic rhetoric and proposed that preachers of a new homiletic pay more attention to the sermon's *eventfulness*— "not so much what the sermon 'is' as what the sermon 'does' "[38] other, more postmodern paradigms of preaching have been advanced. These include approaches of induction, indirection, narrative and story, imaging of thematic moves, and efforts to explore the semantics of a post-Christendom identity. But whatever the approaches, they all appear to share two features: (1) a common discontent with the old paradigm in which an overly rationalistic logic of argumentation served as the basis of sermon invention and arrangement; and (2) a productive unity in their serious attention to what occurs in the *event* and through the *language* of preaching.

The discontent with the old rhetorical homiletic is readily documented in contemporary homiletic literature[39] and, in an essay in which he is one of the authors, Bob has already attempted to identify the productive unity found among the approaches to preaching collectively labeled as the New Homiletics.[40] We will continue to pursue this question at various points in this book, but for now we would suggest that most of the strategies of preaching that have been proposed in the last quarter of the twentieth century are all still reacting, in part, to a previous genera-tion's overemphasis on *logos*. Many of the approaches that have been labeled the New Homiletics have distanced themselves from *logos* by emphasizing *pathos* in their interest to create an affective experience for listeners. Some of the newer, postliberal, post-Christendom approaches to preaching have responded by dis-tancing themselves from *logos* and *pathos*. They tend to place greater emphasis on *ethos* in an effort to help listeners rediscover and affirm the character of their true identity as a community of faith.[41] Homiletics has been enriched by these efforts to explore new ways to preach the gospel. But the observant reader will have already guessed that part of our purpose here is to challenge preachers to adopt a rhetorical stance that finds an appropriate balance in the tensional relationship between rhetoric's means of persuasion.

The homileticians who first voiced their discontent with a pre-vious generation's overemphasis of *logos* were largely unaware of the way in which nineteenth century homiletics had embraced the rationalism of Enlightenment rhetoric. Nor were they aware that contemporary rhetorical theory had *not* remained fixed in Whately's rhetorical theory, but was going through its own para-digm shift.[42] What becomes obvious is that homiletics during the third quarter of the twentieth century was rejecting a rhetoric that was already a petrified artifact? Rhetoric, like theology, biblical studies, and liturgics, is a historic discipline whose current enter-prise will always be affected by the reigning philosophical incli-nations of its day. For example, our presentation of the art of rhetoric in this book will reflect this necessary, and occasionally, we hope, productive inclination. But it is also time for preachers to acknowledge anew what Broadus rightly called the "kindred relationship" between rhetoric and homiletics.

FURTHERING THE CONVERSATION

In the chapters that follow, we have chosen to use the classic Aristotelian trivium of treating invention, style, and arrangement as guides for our discussion, with separate chapters devoted to each of the three inventional means of persuasion: *ethos, pathos,* and *logos.* We intend to present rhetorical theory in a way that helps preachers recognize its immediate relevance so that they will want to discover how to adopt a rhetorical stance in preaching. We agree that preaching is more than a rhetorical art. However, in the name of reclaiming the relevance of biblical studies, theology, and liturgics for a revitalized homiletic theory, we resist the reactionary position that would shuffle rhetoric off to the children's table, as if it has little more than mechanics to add to the conversation at the adult table. Whether we bring Aristotle, Cicero, and Quintilian into the conversation, or modern rhetoricians like Campbell and Booth, we hope it will become evident that, in answer to the question, "When did all this get started?" we are inviting modern preachers to become participants in a conversation that has been occurring for as long as preachers have been reflecting on what they are going to say this week.

On Preaching "Truth"

In a graduate seminar class on medieval rhetoric Bob recalls the assignment of a paper to take a position on whether Augustine's *On Christian Doctrine* is actually "a rhetoric." For a book to be a formal "rhetoric" it has to apply the principles and assumptions of the art of rhetoric to the subject matter of one of the human sciences.[43] Most of us took a position that, *of course it was a rhetoric. It must be if it is anthologized in so many histories of rhetoric.* But then came the challenge: if rhetoric has always been an exercise in the art of persuasion relevant to matters about which the truth cannot be known (re: matters open to dispute), then *On Christian Doctrine* fails to meet the criteria because Augustine wanted to use it to persuade people to accept "truth." According to this position, the work is not a rhetoric because it fails one of the primary tests of the art's assumptions.

Where the subject matter of rhetoric is the *probable* and *plausible* and the subject matter of the philosopher using logic is *demonstrable truth,* early Christian homilies assumed that the subject matter of the Christian message was *revealed truth* (cf.

1 Cor. 2:1-5). Many Christians from the time of Augustine until the present have stumbled over using an art that tries to persuade, especially when the person preaching believes that they are preaching *revealed truth*. For many it seems like a fundamental contradiction or a slide down a slippery slope into relativism.

● QUESTIONS FOR GROUP DISCUSSION

Take a position. Should preaching be about making plausible arguments in support of the probable understanding of faith or valid arguments in support of faith's revealed truths? In taking a position you may need to make a prior decision as to whether you believe (1) argument/persuasion has a role in preaching, or (2) preaching should try to avoid persuasion altogether and simply be willing to inform only those "who have ears to hear" about the "truth" of the gospel? Be prepared to defend your position with others.

On Getting the Historical Metaphor Right

In chapter 1 we noted that some homileticians have used the metaphor of marriage to describe the relationship between rhetoric and homiletics. In this chapter we have noted and made cautious use of Broadus' metaphor of a "kindred" relationship and we have also made use of the metaphor of an "ongoing conversation."

● QUESTIONS FOR GROUP DISCUSSION

Which of these metaphors do you prefer? Or do you have one of your own invention? In light of the discussion in this chapter, be prepared to defend your preference in a group discussion.

READ MORE ABOUT IT

Aristotle. *On Rhetoric: A Theory of Civic Discourse.* Newly translated, with introduction, notes, and appendices by George Kennedy. Oxford: Oxford University Press, 1991.

George A. Kennedy. *A New History of Classical Rhetoric.* Princeton: Princeton University Press, 1994.

Richard Lischer, ed. *Theories of Preaching: Selected Readings in the Homiletical Tradition.* Durham, N.C.: Labyrinth Press, 1987.

Paul Scott Wilson. *A Concise History of Preaching.* Nashville: Abingdon Press, 1992.

Chapter 3

Who Do They Think I Am?

You have heard, no doubt, of my earlier life in Judaism. I was violently persecuting the church of God and was trying to destroy it
> —The Apostle Paul, Galatians 1:13

If there's a clear and distinguishing feature about the process of leading, it's in the distinction between mobilizing others to do and mobilizing others to *want* to do. People in positions of authority can get other people to do something because of the power they wield, but leaders mobilize others to *want* to act because of the credibility they have.... Leaders sustain the requisite credibility by their actions—challenging, inspiring, enabling, modeling and encouraging.
> —James M. Kouzes and Barry Z. Posner, *The Leadership Challenge*[1]

EMPTY VESSEL?

ONE CAN ONLY imagine the reaction of Jewish Christians when they heard that Saul, their once feared persecutor, had begun to preach the good news! Their astonishment, amazement, and perhaps skepticism, seem only to be matched by Paul's own amazement at the turn that his life had taken. As he wrote to the church in Galatia, "The one who formerly was persecuting us is now proclaiming the faith he once tried to destroy" (Gal. 1:23). How could it be that this one time opponent of the church was now one of its greatest proponents? Could, and should, they trust him?

In the opening of his letter to the churches in Galatia, Paul devotes a great deal of energy to establishing *ethos*, or credibility and authority. Who is Paul and why should the Christians in

Galatia listen to him? These questions had become important again because "some" had begun proclaiming "a gospel contrary to what you received [from me]" (Gal. 1:9).

This question of his authority was an issue that dogged his heels throughout his ministry. He argues that his authority ultimately comes not from human sources, but from divine revelation. "The gospel that was proclaimed by me is not of human origin; for I did not receive it from a human source, nor was I taught it, but I received it through a revelation of Jesus Christ" (Gal. 1:11-12). Was that enough? Apparently not, since Paul proceeds to establish his *Ivy League* credentials.

He does not try to ignore or cover up his former life. Rather, he reminds his readers that he was once their enemy. For a people who prize repentance and new life, this becomes a powerful authorization, "I once was lost, but now I'm found." But Paul also knows that his former "sinfulness" is not enough to confirm him as an trustworthy preacher. Consequently, he stresses both his educational accomplishments and religious fervor. He had been a child prodigy, skipping grades, graduating early; "I advanced in Judaism beyond many among my people of the same age" (Gal. 1:14). And, in spite of the fact that a principal purpose of the letter was to rebut those who would stress the primacy of Jewish Christianity, he lifts up his Jewishness, "I was far more zealous for the traditions of my ancestors" (Gal. 1:14). He was chosen from his mother's womb, visited by Jesus Christ, educated in Arabia, and became a successful missionary. All of these, Paul believes, are plausible arguments for accepting him as a credible source of authority. Similarly, at the end of the letter to the Galatians, Paul is thrown back on *ethos*: "See what large letters I make when I am writing in my own hand" (Gal. 6:11). More than just his arguments, he has interrupted his dictation to put his own hand to seal his words. There should be no question about the authority behind his letter. It is he, Paul, who is writing to convince them of the necessity of oneness in Christ. Not surprisingly, this issue of character was essential to authority in the era in which Aristotle could say that "there are three things we trust other than logical demonstration: practical wisdom *(phronesis)* and virtue *(arete)* and good will *(eunoia)*."[2] In other words, we trust wise counsel *(logos)* from an individual of good character *(ethos)*.

Our newspapers and television programs are often devoted to demonstrating the frailties of those in power. Charges of sexual or financial misconduct, whether currently or in one's distant past, provide sensational headlines and often bring down those who, otherwise, seem to be competently fulfilling their duties. The lives of presidents, generals, doctors, and yes, clergy, are all subject to this intense scrutiny. In fact, the more highly placed the individual the more extreme the scrutiny. "Is this," we demand to know, "a good person whom we can trust to carry out important duties?" If a person's *private* actions are questionable, can we trust his or her *public* actions?

And when it comes to preaching this is even more pressing. The Word became flesh, and it continues to be from flesh to flesh, earthen vessel to earthen vessel, *ethos* to *ethos*, that the good news is announced. Aristotle said that, of the three means of persuasion, "Character is almost, . . . the controlling factor in persuasion."[3] Bob came to appreciate this when he was the pastor in a small community. Walking down the streets of that town on any day of the week, most people would tip their head or hat and greet him with a "Hello Pastor Reid." At first, he did not know many people beyond his own congregation, but most people, regardless of their congregation, knew who he was. He had no anonymity in that community and life was very different from his next pastorate in a city where he was almost wholly anonymous whenever he left the church building.

Sometimes the primacy of *ethos* is unfair. We are aware of a pastor who was involved in an accident, hitting a young person who stepped between two cars. The young person died as a result of the accident. The authorities determined that the pastor was not at fault. There was little or nothing he could have done to avoid the outcome. It really *was* an accident. None of this changed the community perception that it was a pastor who was involved in this accident. Attendance at the church stagnated. Was it because the incident became associated with the ministry? We do know that the pastor eventually chose to relocate in another state where there would be no community memory of this incident. For those of us who preach, the personal character and identity, our *ethos*, is fundamental to whether or not the message we preach will be accepted or rejected.

In this chapter we will explore the rhetorical nature of *ethos*. How do character and authority function as rhetorical strategies and choices in preaching? How does character as revealed in the sermon contribute to or influence the relationship between the preacher and the congregation? What are the ethics of establishing credibility within the sermon itself?

CHARACTER AND AUTHORITY

Think, for a moment, about a recent visit to the doctor. The doctor's office wall was probably filled with diplomas and credentials that displayed where the doctor had attended medical school and trained in her specialized field. Did you find yourself squinting to read the fine print? Just when was this training anyway, and did she receive any special awards? If this person is going to be taking care of your body you want to make sure that she earned good grades. The same experience no doubt occurred when you last took your car to the garage. Had the mechanic been through the proper, award-winning training? Credentials are important. They are, however, not determinative. If the words your doctor uses, the way she uses them, or her voice, facial expression, gestures, or body language are disconcerting, credentials will probably prove insufficient. The diploma may read *Harvard*, but if the doctor seems confused or unsure, or if the doctor has no "bedside manner," we suspect you will not return because you won't trust her, no matter what the diplomas say.

Lucy became aware of the complex nature of *ethos* and its establishment when she began to preach. In spite of the fact that she had graduated from one of the seminaries of the church and had been duly ordained by a bishop in the church, her gender presented a stumbling block for some people. There were numerous occasions when people actually refused to listen to her or to acknowledge that she had the authority to speak. But she also came to appreciate that there were other occasions when people, who would not accept the church's authority to ordain women, were "won over" by her *ethos*—her ability to present herself as a capable and credible witness to the gospel of Jesus Christ. We judge people's *ethos*, or character, every day, whether it is in the doctor's office, the mechanic's garage, or in the pulpit. We make those judgments through a process so subtle that we could never fully explain it.

Early teachers of rhetoric were aware of both the complexity and centrality of this process of judgment both in giving and in listening to speeches. Classical rhetorical theory was founded upon the assumption that the listener was a thinking, reasoning, decision-making individual who retained the right to be, or not to be, persuaded. They were all too aware that one could make the clearest arguments in the most elegant manner, yet, if the audience remained unconvinced that the speaker was a knowledgeable, virtuous person who had their best interests at heart, it would be almost impossible to persuade them.

Two issues, therefore, were of supreme importance: the character and the authority of the speaker. While these often appear as synonyms for *ethos*, it is crucial to see how these are two different concepts that function quite differently. The Greek understanding of *ethos* was that of character or virtue. It was imperative that a speaker demonstrate to his listeners that he (and it usually was a he) was worthy of their trust. A good speaker, according to Aristotle, was one who could convince his listeners that he was virtuous, had common sense, and had the best interest of his listener at heart. The Greeks had two schools of thought about this notion of the virtue of an orator. One school, known as *sophistic*, primarily stressed the need of the speaker to construct a virtuous character, or persona, within the speech. The other school, practiced by the students of Isocrates, stressed the necessity of training in what it meant to be a virtuous citizen. Only then, they argued, could true virtue be reflected in their speeches. So one school focused on how to *construct the persona* of a virtuous character while the other taught their students how *to be* a virtuous citizen.

Three centuries later, when the Greek word *ethos* was translated into the Latin language and Roman culture, they did not use a word that meant character or virtue. Rather, *ethos* became *auctoritas*, the word for authority. More than his good sense or goodwill, a speaker needed to demonstrate by what power he had been given the permission to speak. With that change, the validation moved from *internal* virtues to *external* authority. Authority was not necessarily something that one cultivated through long years of virtuous habits. Instead, it was conferred on one by a representative of an external institution. One's character could be less than stellar, but, if one had been granted authority then one had the *ethos* to speak.

By focusing more on external structural authority than on moral character or virtue, speakers were often able to deflect questions of character. Rather than having to convince an audience to listen, it was assumed that the audience would listen because of a position that was held by the speaker. This became an important issue within the early church, growing within the Hellenistic culture that was a synthesis of Greek and Roman cultures.

Preachers have always struggled with the primacy of external *ethos* versus the necessity to establish internal *ethos* in what they say. Frequently, preachers neglect the development of *ethos* within the sermon believing that their authority to preach has already been established and accepted by their listeners based on the virtue of their call and/or ordination. Consequently, much of the *ethos* of the sermon is often developed by default. The question of external *ethos*, over and against internal *ethos*—character developed within the sermon itself—may be one of the most crucial questions for preachers today. This is increasingly a factor in situations where the status of ordination or the necessity of a "call" may no longer be enough to provide a foundation for or an authority for preaching.

It is our assumption that the question of the development of *ethos* should be treated as a both/and rather than an "either/or" question. We need to include both an emphasis on external authority while returning to more of an intentional emphasis on character that is developed within the sermon itself. In the next section we will consider how *ethos* is developed outside of the sermon. We will then turn to an examination of how a preacher constructs a favorable persona within the sermon itself. Only after we have considered these two dimensions will we be able to explore *ethos* as a fundamental element in a constructive theology of preaching.

EXTERNAL ETHOS: DEVELOPING ETHOS OUTSIDE THE SERMON

Even before a preacher speaks a word, the congregation has already begun the complicated and complex process of judging. Will they or won't they listen to what the preacher has to say? Will they respond to the preacher's call to repent or serve God? And, even if they agree and say that they will, will they eventually do what they have said they would do? *Ethos* is developed, in part, outside of the actual text and delivery of the sermon in several ways. However, we must not equate external *ethos* with authority alone, for external *ethos* also begins with development of the character of the preacher.

We had a very lively discussion over these issues while writing this chapter. Lucy was both raised and ordained in the Episcopal church, and Bob became a Christian during college and is an ordained Baptist minister. What is normative for an Episcopalian is often problematic in a Baptist church, and *vice versa*. Consequently, as you read about the various ways that one might establish *ethos*, you need to be aware just as we became aware, that conceptions of *ethos* are culturally shaped. So, we need to be attentive to the differences that exist between traditions. Perhaps more than in any other section of our book, differences in confessional traditions will show up here. What we have attempted to do is to begin to suggest some of the broad categories that are used to establish *ethos*. You, as the reader, must enter into our conversation and translate these categories into your church's theology and its cultural practice.

Nurturing the Preacher:
Developing Ethos Through Character

Nurturing Virtue. Earlier we noted one of the significant debates that engaged Greek rhetoricians. Where Aristotle argued that *ethos* was established both prior to and within the speech, Isocrates, his principal competitor, stressed that a person became an excellent speaker principally by being a virtuous, well-rounded individual. Virtue mattered for both philosophers, but Isocrates made it a prerequisite to mastery of the art. For his part, Aristotle reluctantly admitted that virtue could be feigned by a speaker if audiences were ignorant of the facts. Eventually, the debate was reduced to the Latin maxim that defined the art of oratory: *vir bonus dicendi peritus*—"the good man speaking well."[4] Where Aristotle had argued for the primacy of character among the "means" of persuasion, later rhetoricians sided with Isocrates and simply reduced the whole art to a mixture of good character and mastery of technique. Either way, orators learned that no matter how hard they worked to craft what they wanted to say, listeners would still be influenced strongly, perhaps over-whelmingly, by how they viewed the speaker as a person. Thus, who we are is an inescapable part of what gets communicated when we stand up to speak.

Technically, Aristotelian ethos refers more to the kind of *character* we construct for ourselves with our words. But rhetoric has traditionally called for more than the strict Aristotelian notion of technical ethos. For inherent in the definition of "the good man speaking well" is the necessity of civic virtue. Therefore, a preacher needs to be attentive to the way that he or she establishes *ethos* within the sermon, a subject we will take up in the next section. At this point we would merely add that Aristotle might have argued that ethos is primarily about the character we construct in what gets said, but he would have wholeheartedly affirmed that listeners should only believe arguments put forward by a person of good character. Disreputable people are not to be believed regardless of whether their arguments are cogent, their passion is real, or their credentials are extraordinary. Virtue matters.[5]

More than a century ago Phillips Brooks offered a definition of preaching that tried to maintain this same balance between what gets said and who says it. In what is arguably the most famous statement ever professed in the *Yale Lectures on Preaching*, Brooks declared that "preaching is the bringing of truth through personality."[6] There are many today who would debate the emphasis on the *personal* in this pronouncement. For example, preachers who have been deeply affected by the neoorthodox movement would argue that the presence of the preacher in sermons is intrusive, drawing attention to the speaker rather than to the transcendent presence of God. But what is the alternative? Depersonalized sermons? Or the artifice that never acknowledges how much the person of the speaker shapes what gets said? In a reaffirmation of Brooks's original statement, Susan Hedahl has claimed that, "Undoubtedly, the central response to any sermon emerges from the listeners' perception that preachers either do or do not believe in their own witness. Parishioner interaction with the preacher and parish life during the rest of the week will only confirm the judgment. Whatever the shape of the sermon, congregational responses exhibit the truth of Aristotle's observation: *Who* preaches is the most essential component for the receptivity of the Gospel."[7] Virtue does matter.

As leaders, preachers must do more than share the vision and enable others to act. They also have a responsibility to model the way. Leaders set the example by behaving in ways that are consistent with the shared values of their community of faith.[8] In most religious communities, those values are also an expression of the community's belief in a transcendent God who calls people to responsible and ethical behavior. Preachers who are unwilling to model the way of faith in their personal conduct will not be perceived as credible interpreters of the faith. Political leaders may try to argue that their wisdom in governance is separate from their wisdom in private morality, but parishioners will understandably look to the preacher to be a responsible leader in the journey toward accepting the ethical claims of the gospel. Of course our listeners know our frailties as well, if not better than, we do. Yet Christian leaders who preach the gospel have always been called to strive for personal virtue because virtue matters in the proclamation of the gospel. When participants in a community of faith see the continuity between the sermons and the authentic engagement of the minister in nurturing his or her own life of faith, they are more likely to become engaged in the vision of nurturing their own life of faith.

Nurturing the Life of Reflection. We agree with Craddock that a preacher must also be attentive to developing and nurturing the "life of study."[9] A congregation responds favorably to a preacher's keen intelligence, big heart, and plain, old common sense. These are qualities developed slowly and conscientiously over time. They are habits of the heart and mind, cultivated through extensive reading, sensitive and compassionate involvement in the lives of the congregation and community, and prayer.

An enlivening preacher knows that reading novels, short stories, and the newspaper, and catching some of the more provocative television programs and movies are not a waste of time. They connect the preacher with the world in which the congregation lives, providing a common context in which to frame the issues of the day. Only by reading classic and contemporary expressions of the dilemmas of the human condition can a preacher learn to embed subtexts within the canvas of a sermon. Subtexts provide bridges of connection for listeners. This is equally true whether the subtext is the way the New Testament takes up the story of Abraham or David, or the way Jesus' story becomes subtext in the "Aha!" of a contemporary story. Consider the way Flannery O'Connor told the story of our own painful awakening to God's presence in our lives in "Revelation." In this short story Mrs. Tupin finds herself demanding of God "Who do you think you are?" and sometimes, so do we. Then, as in John's version of "Revelation," we suddenly grasp just who God is.[10] Aristotle called this use of subtext, "the joy of recognition." The ability to weave subtext into our sermons only comes about as we listen to life through scripture and the other human arts.[11]

Furthermore, reading and learning extensively in various fields informs and challenges the preacher's ulitimate goals: biblical studies, theology, and spirituality.

Other Kinds of External Ethos

Professional Credentials. Very few Christian communities allow just anyone to preach during a worship service. While there is a continuum of authorization from strict exclusivity, requiring ordination through a system of licensing, to a more inclusive view where the invitation of the pastor or congregation is enough, there is usually some way that communities control access to the pulpit. Some church traditions pride themselves on viewing the preacher as one of the brothers or sisters who is set aside for the task of preaching, but who holds no honor above anyone else in this role, while other church traditions view seminary training and ordination as normative. One may preach as a seminarian or a licensed lay speaker, but these are the exceptions that prove the rule.

However, once the individual congregation or a wider denominational structure has granted permission, the preacher has a variety of means of demonstrating the fact that prior authorization has been given. The Reverend before a person's name, in addition to an honorific of respect, is one way of establishing prior *ethos*. When the congregation looks at the bulletin and finds the preacher's name beside "Sermon," and the preacher's name is preceded by the title The Rev., not only will they have certain expectations about what the preacher will say, and how he or she will say it, they also assume that the preacher received appropriate training and approval for speaking to the community.

Stepping into the pulpit, or some other designated "preaching space," is another way that the preacher signals those in the congregation that she or he has been granted the authority to preach. This signals authority, while also establishing the nature of the preacher's relationship with the congregation. It was no mistake that pulpits became the central focal points in Protestant churches that stressed the importance of the preached word. Their height not only demanded attention, but also forced the congregation to "look up" to the preacher. The preacher's location within the worship space was an indication that he was, during the moment of the sermon, not a fellow traveler with the congregation, but God's herald. Consequently, modern preachers, whose theology of preaching and ordination have changed to a more horizontal understanding, often feel uncomfortable climbing the stairs of those pulpits and looking down at the tops of their parishioners' heads. They prefer to stand in and among the congregation, enacting this alternate theology of ministry.

Appearance. The physical appearance of preachers is another way that they communicate their relationship with the congregation and enhance *ethos*. While we often remind our children that one cannot judge a book by its cover, the reality is that we do, in fact, do just that.

One cover that we judge, for example, is the preacher's clothing. In some church traditions there is an expectation that the preacher will wear a robe, while in other traditions, robing is viewed as anathema. While we might be tempted to say that not wearing a robe allows the preacher more freedom, as someone who preaches in both of these communities, Bob observes that the opposite is true. When robing is not an expectation, the choice to robe always involves a question of the perception of authority associated with robing. When one robes, the Roman notion of authority is ever present. Robes mark the clergy as set apart and ordained to the task. When robing is discouraged, the character of one's personal *ethos*, both external and internal, is far more explicit. For example, when he preaches under the auspices of authority, symbolized by the robe, Bob notes that he feels greater freedom to express his own opinion without having somehow "to authorize" it from a biblical text. In part, the robe symbolizes the recognition that there is a sacred tradition apart from the preacher who may have personal opinions that are somewhat at variance with the tradition which has granted that authority. Unrobed, Bob notes that he is much more dependent on his own presentation of what the Bible says. There is no symbol that immediately authorizes the interpretation, and the congregation is more apt to weigh what they believe to be the biblical authorization of the pronouncements. When robed, the authority of the preacher is authorized by the tradition that grants those who wear such vestments to speak for God. Unrobed, the authority of the preacher is authorized by his or her singular faithfulness in preaching the text.

Lucy, on the other hand, has experienced the profound effect that robes have on helping to establish her *ethos*. Unlike most Episcopal clergy, she does not wear a clerical collar. Consequently, when she arrives at a new church to conduct services she is unrecognizable as a clergyperson. She regularly experiences the difference in the way people treat her once they meet her again in her vestments. The alb and stole proclaim to the people in the church that the broader church approves of the ordination of women and has granted her the authority to preach the Word and celebrate the sacraments. A robe or alb also suppresses individual differences, stressing, instead, the continuity of the office enacting Paul's admonition that, in Christ we are neither male nor female, for both women and men wear the same type of garment.

Introductions. Preachers are also aware of the difference between preaching to a congregation week after week and preaching to a congregation that they have never met before. In the first instance, as the congregation prepares to listen to the preacher, an ongoing relationship precedes and informs the sermon. They come filled with expectations, one hopes favorable, and it is within the context of that relationship that a preacher preaches the sermon.

However, there are many times when the congregation does not know the preacher. It may be the preacher's first Sunday in a new congregation, a pulpit exchange, or an invitation to preside over a special event in the life of the congregation. In those instances additional information may be helpful, information that goes beyond the wearing of a stole or a name in the bulletin. In those instances introductions, whether spoken or written, are another way that a preacher establishes *ethos* prior to the delivery of the sermon. If we think back to Paul's missionary efforts, Paul's reputation had, unfortunately, preceded him. We suspect that he often had to search out someone who would be willing to provide a good introduction, whose *ethos* he could initially borrow in assuring his Jewish Christian listeners that he came as a friend rather than a foe. Introductions can have a powerful influence on a congregation. Therefore, think carefully what you want to have written or said about you before you preach.

INTERNAL ETHOS:
DEVELOPING ETHOS WITHIN THE SERMON

Aristotle considered *ethos,* along with *logos,* and *pathos,* to be internal or artistic *(entechnoi)* proofs. By artistic he meant proofs that were created by the speaker for that particular speech. Artistic proofs were contrasted with nonartistic or external proofs *(atechnoi).* Nonartistic proofs were pieces of evidence that a speaker used, "they are not provided by 'us' [that is, the potential speaker] but are preexisting."[12] These included the testimony of witnesses, written contracts, and testimony extracted under torture. Though often powerful, Aristotle argued that nonartistic proofs were, none the less, unreliable. A speaker could only *use* nonartistic proofs, while a speaker could *invent* artistic proofs. So invented proofs offer more control. Therefore, a preacher who relied only upon her authority and credibility as a "proof" established by external sources would likely be perceived more as, say, a denominational spokesperson. On the other hand, a preacher who relied as much, if not more, upon her ability to create or invent her *ethos* within the sermon would be more likely to be perceived as a preacher of good news who happens to be authorized to speak.[13]

Creation of a Persona

How, exactly, does one invent, or create, a credible *ethos?* Perhaps it is more helpful if we think of this as a persona or role that the preacher develops and establishes during the sermon. This persona is being developed whether or not the preacher is consciously involved in its development. It is crucial, therefore, that we think about what "self" we want and need to present to our listeners, and then consider the choices we must make rhetorically to demonstrate that persona.

We might be tempted to argue that we should have only *one*

self, but we know that our one self is really a conglomeration of many selves. Lucy is wife, mother, daughter, professor, preacher, and Bob is husband, father, son, brother, professor, pastor. Each of these roles demands that we interact with people differently. The way that Lucy speaks to her husband, or the way that Bob speaks with his daughter or son, cannot, nor should not, be the way they speak to their students. As the situation changes and the audience changes, so does the role. A preacher recognizes that one Sunday calls for a more pastoral tone, while the next Sunday may see the preacher stepping into the persona of teacher, and the next Sunday calling for a prophet. Preaching textbooks frequently describe the various personas available to preachers. Thomas Long, for example, argues that there are three master metaphors: herald, pastor, or storyteller.[14] The problem, therefore, is deciding which role to employ and when.

In other words, one's persona is created through a variety of elements in the sermon. We create that role by the arguments we make, our stylistic choices, the words we choose, the "tone" of our language, the metaphors and illustrations we employ, and the cluster of elements that make up the performance of our sermon: voice, body language, gestures, and facial expression. All of these create an impression of who we are in our listener's mind. We create a role that will leave our listeners favorably disposed to listening to and agreeing with us.

The preacher may be the kindest, holiest, or most spirit-filled servant of God, however, the preacher must still demonstrate that role or persona by employing appropriate "credibility devices" within the sermon. In a study of "successful" and "unsuccessful" Baptist preachers, the language choices of preachers were compared to their church's growth and financial vigor. The sermons of successful preachers were "more personal, more narrational, more assured, and more detailed," while the sermons preached in churches that were experiencing a decline "used more passive constructions, less interesting language, and a less businesslike, more folksy style." Another study observed "that highly credible speakers used more human interest language, a richer vocabulary, a more concrete style, and less cumbersome sentence structures."[15]

The role or persona that a speaker chooses is ultimately linked to the speaker's often unconscious theory of how communication works. One critic has identified seven "implicit views of communication" and the persona that is associated with each theory.[16] If one has a *magical* theory, then one will adopt the persona of the master wizard, the one who reveals the hidden secrets and knows more than everyone else. If one has a *mechanical* theory of communication, the speaker is the physician who is diagnosing societal maladies. The *experiential* theory implies the persona of a storyteller and the *rationalistic* theory the persona of a scientific expert. Speakers who have a *parental* theory see themselves as patient, but hierarchically dominating authority figures. *Antagonistic* theory calls forth the persona of the crusader ready to do battle with the perceived enemy. For them, submission is the only end, there is no possibility of compromise. Finally, one might have a *formulaic* theory of communication, which implies the persona of the expert who is the inspirational motivator.

Each of these theories can be very effective. None of them are wrong. However, the preacher needs to understand that each theory represents both a persona and an implicit view of communication evoked by that persona. One's theory of communication says a great deal about one's theology of preaching, whether intended or not. In fact, it is possible that the persona a preacher tends to adopt could functionally deny the theology of preaching she espouses.

Authenticity

This last idea naturally raises the question of authenticity and the ethics of establishing credibility within the sermon itself. Is a congregation able to "read" an authentic connection between the persona developed within the sermon and the person of the preacher who meets them everyday? When we say that a preacher must intentionally create a role within the sermon, this certainly does not mean that a preacher can create a persona that is at odds with his or her personality. We are not manipulating the congregation. Rather, we are entering into a relationship of mutual respect and concern. And, central to the understanding of *ethos* and the part that it plays in the persuasive enterprise, is the recognition that ultimately it is the audience, or congregation, who decides if the speaker is believable, credible, and speaks with conviction. Does this preacher really care about the gospel? Does this preacher care about the congregation, before, during, and after the sermon?

It is within the question of authenticity that we link the internal and external dimensions of *ethos* with character and authority. But this is complicated by the realization that character and virtue are, in part, culturally determined. The preacher who demonstrates authenticity is the preacher who knows and understands the community to whom she or he is preaching. Only then will the preacher know what virtues to lift up and demonstrate. Paul recognized that repentance and conversion were counted as virtues within the early Christian community. Aristotle's Greek *polis* prized common sense and virility. What virtues do we value today?

A contemporary textbook on rhetorical criticism suggests that modern speakers must demonstrate that they are powerful, competent, trustworthy, have goodwill, high ideals, and can identify with their audience.[17] But what is the relationship between authority and authenticity? Authority, according to theologian Bernard Lonergan, which is legitimate power, ultimately grounds its source of power in cooperation, and the carrier of power is the community. Authority is not in the individual. Rather, it is within the community. This, Lonergan argues demands a change in the virtues which a religious communicator must demonstrate. Classical rhetorical theory offered an account of the qualities that a speaker needed, such as good sense, goodwill, and virtue. Lonergan suggests a contemporary account of authenticity. One, according to Lonergan, must demonstrate that one is attentive, intelligent, reasonable, and responsible. Likewise, Lonergan asserts that preachers who seem inattentive, obtuse, unreasonable, and irresponsible, will have a difficult time winning congregations' trust.

When we are attentive, intelligent, reasonable, and responsible, Lonergan argues, we are authentic: "Authenticity makes power legitimate ... [and] confers on power the aura and prestige of authority." Without authenticity, we will have no authority, only naked power. What's more, Lonergan notes, authenticity "is reached only by long and sustained fidelity to the transcendental precepts [attentiveness, intelligence, reasonableness, responsibility]."[18]

Performance

Classical rhetorical theory often referred to the "canon." According to the canon, when one spoke, one needed to do five things. One needed to *invent* the arguments, then *arrange* them in the proper order. One then had to choose an appropriate *style*, and *memorize* the speech. Finally one had to *deliver* the speech. It is here in our discussion of *ethos* and our authenticity that we turn to this essential part of the canon—the delivery or performance of our sermons. We mentioned earlier in this section that *ethos* is created through the tone of voice, body language, facial expressions, and gestures. Performance and delivery, therefore, encompass more than clarity and loudness. They are the enactment of one's *ethos*, one's believability and credibility, that is, humanness. Does one come across as imperious and condescending, or accessible and respectful? Listeners determine our credibility by what they "hear" in our tone of voice, and observe in our facial expression, in the way we stand, and in the way we move our body. Emotional integrity and dramatic consistency are central to the effective *ethos*.[19]

Personal Illustrations

Finally, we will examine the relationship between the creation of a convincing persona and the use of personal illustrations. As we indicated above, this is a subject of disagreement among homileticians. Some theorists argue against their use,[20] while others argue that narcissism is not the alternative to efforts to depersonalize the sermon.[21] Objections to the uses of personal illustration range from reactions to misuses on one hand to the Barthian rejection of all attempts to make gospel "relevant." Whatever the reason, we believe they arise from an incomplete understanding of the indispensable contribution of *ethos* to any rhetorical undertaking.

Ultimately, there are two options open to speakers. They may take either a prominent or a diminished authorial status.[22] The first is an approach in which the author plays a central and very up-front role. Throughout this chapter we have been referring to Paul's letter to the church in Galatia. In that, as well as his other letters, Paul had prominent authorial status. In those letters we know who the author is, what he is like, and what his views are. In texts that adopt a prominent authorial status, the author's style, tone, identity, and passion, perform a crucial persuasive function.

This rhetoric may be contrasted with the cool, objective, detached rhetoric that adopts a diminished authorial status. If we read a scientific work, or even some systematic theology, we know very little about the author. However, while the author may not establish *ethos* through the use of personal illustrations or reflections, we must not fall into the trap of thinking that the author is not creating a role or persona. Persona is always there, whether represented as impartial, unbiased, or expert.

Each of these approaches creates a persona which functions in different ways. The decision is a choice that preachers must make, "Personal passion or aloof control? The difference is not unimportant."[23] Will a preacher be a prominent figure within the sermon, or adopt a self-effacing and remote presence?

FURTHERING THE CONVERSATION

We have come full circle. We began this chapter by noting the tension between character and authority in classical rhetoric and Pauline theology. Now contemporary rhetorical theory and contemporary theology once again drive us to rethink and revisit this vital tension. We cannot speak or preach unless we recognize the power of the community to grant us authority, and they will not grant us authority unless we are able to demonstrate that we are virtuous and worthy of their respect. As you consider the importance of *ethos* within the theology of preaching, we hope that this chapter has stimulated a number of questions and challenged your thinking. While we certainly cannot begin to address all of those questions, we will point to three significant issues that we believe require our attention.

The Ever Present Self

Rhetoric seeks to remind us of the importance of *ethos*. The *who* our listeners determine we are is essential to our presentations and the arguments that we are making because it convinces our listeners that they should be listening to us. Therefore, we must recognize that there is always a self being presented.

• QUESTIONS FOR GROUP DISCUSSION

Some preaching textbooks argue that personal references should be eliminated from sermons so that the focus of preaching will be Christ and not ourselves. Is this possible or even desirable? Does rhetorical attention to the self we present to our listeners imply that we are not being attentive to Christ?

Creation of a Persona

When we recognize the primacy of *ethos* within the preaching project, we must begin to recognize the importance of attending to and establishing our *ethos* both within and without the sermon. All too often this is done by default. The preacher is not aware of the need to deliberately create a persona within the sermon or see the connection between preaching and the life of study. Therefore, rhetoric helps us to attend to the choices we must make.

• QUESTION FOR GROUP DISCUSSION

We have discussed the importance of authenticity of the preacher and the creation of a persona within the sermon. How do we reconcile our person and the persona we create?

Ethos: A Relational Process

Many mistakenly believe that the classical understanding of *ethos* focuses only on the speaker. It is the speaker who is virtuous. It is the speaker who possesses the proper credentials for speaking. They overlook the importance of the audience in this equation. The relationship and conversation between the preacher and listener, therefore, become crucial issues as we begin the process of developing an understanding of the role *ethos* performs in a theology of preaching. *Ethos*, a process of negotiation, does not ignore the listener. Rather, it sends us into a relationship with the community.

• QUESTION FOR GROUP DISCUSSION

If we say that ethos is the self in relationship and conversation with the listener, with whom are you in conversation and how do you carry on that conversation?

READ MORE ABOUT IT

Charles L. Bartow. *God's Human Speech: A Practical Theology of Proclamation.* Grand Rapids: William B. Eerdmans, 1997.

Edwina Hunter. "The Preacher as a Social Being in the Community of Faith," in *Preaching as a Social Act: Theology and Practice*, ed. Arthur Van Seters. Nashville: Abingdon Press, 1988.

J. Randall Nichols. *The Restoring Word: Preaching as Pastoral Communication.* San Francisco: Harper & Row, 1987.

Thomas Troeger. *The Parable of Ten Preachers.* Nashville: Abingdon Press, 1992.

Chapter 4

How Will They Come to Care?

Abraham Lincoln said, "When I hear a man preach, I like to see him act as if he were fighting bees." Exuberance has its attractions, but zealous preaching also packs liabilities. Flailing limbs may so dominate the pulpit that the preacher's zeal upstages the sermon's intent. On the other hand, pastors able to weave a literate spell with smooth oratory want to do more than impress a receptive crowd. The art of preaching is not intended to displace the aim: hearts moved to believe in Christ and follow his ways.

—James Berkley, *Preaching to Convince*[1]

"Were not our hearts burning within us while he was talking to us on the road, while he was opening the scriptures to us?"

—An Emmaus disciple, Luke 24:32

ZEAL FOR THE GOSPEL

CLERGY IN THE townships of Massachusetts faced a difficult problem in 1837. Laypeople wanted permission for the abolitionist Grimké sisters to be able to speak in the churches. Congregationalist clergy responded in a "Pastoral Letter" that denounced this "promiscuous activity." For women to speak publicly with men looking on was considered an assault on female character. The letter, which was read and posted in the churches, began by reminding laypeople about a prior decision forbidding itinerant speakers to use the church facilities as a place to raise "perplexing and agitating subjects." In the second half of the letter, the ministers reported their alarm concerning "the dangers which at present seem to threaten the female character with widespread and permanent injury." It disturbed clergy that the *fairer sex* would become so involved in matters of public passion as to "forget themselves ... [and] iterate in the character of public lecturers and teachers." The appropriate exercise of female "enduring influence," they reminded parishioners, was to be exercised in the Sabbath school, in Bible classes, in spiritual graces, in good works, and in a growing acquaintance with the Bible. This was, they concluded, the real "means of a true and safe zeal."[2]

The letter represents just one of the ways past generations sought to circumscribe women's voices. We share the story here because we think the absurd response of calling for *safe zeal* serves as an apt example of just how frightened people can become when confronted with the reality that speakers are able to compel audiences by the passion of their convictions. The Congregational ministers recognized that effective speaking appeals to the listeners' passions as well their rationality, which explains why they believed the Grimké sisters were "forgetting themselves." For what woman of propriety would publicly conduct herself in a manner so as to inflame the passions of men? Of course some men may even have turned out just to see these two women get folk all stirred up. But however odd it may have been to witness a woman speaker, it did not take long for listeners to become persuaded that the issue at stake was not a woman speaking but the dehumanizing experience of slavery. Audiences who departed having heard the Grimké sisters were galvanized to act on their new belief that slavery was an abhorrent evil that must come to an end. Because these sisters cared passionately, their audiences came to care passionately as well.

Passion and zeal disturb many of us; they seem so potentially irrational. We who live in the shadow of the Enlightenment thinkers have come to believe that if changes are to be made in the *status quo*, good people will be moved to act because of good arguments and common sense. Then we recall the images of bodies in Jonestown, the fiery end of the siege at Waco, or even the roar of audiences responding to the emotional appeals of Adolf Hitler. We have reason to distrust efforts to manipulate solely by evoking an emotional response. We should be suspicious of speakers who "play on the emotions" as a means of exercising influence. But, every writer, speaker, and preacher knows that there is nothing more deadly in the art of persuasion then a coldly analytical presentation. When all is said and done, however valid the reasons, if a preacher wants to persuade and move an audience, the listeners need to be able to believe that the preacher cares. Only then are they willing to care as well. Preaching was meant to communicate that which a speaker cares about in a way that helps listeners begin to care as well.

Passionless preaching is deadly dull. If Jesus is the literal ideal of a preacher *homileo*-ing on the road to Emmaus (Luke 24:15), then we need to remember Luke's report that hearts were "burning within" is the ideal response. This is certainly not the last time Luke reports such a powerful response to preaching. Why? Because emotions and feelings are at the very center of our relationship with God and with one another. If safe zeal has any role to play in religion, we are convinced it is not in the pulpit. Preaching the gospel should never be passionless or safe.

We use the term *pathos* to describe the effect emotions and feelings have on an audience as well as the role those emotions play in persuasion. In this chapter we explore ways in which the rhetorical strategy of *pathos* makes use of the passions to affect and *move* listeners. We also discuss the importance of giving imaginative *presence* to the questions or concerns that drive the sermon as an aspect of creating identification. And, finally, we discuss the importance of having an adequate conception of *audience*. These are the concerns of *pathos* relevant to what Aristotle referred to as "disposing the listener in some way."[3]

THE ART OF "DISPOSING THE LISTENER IN SOME WAY"

Take a moment and reflect upon some of the crucial decisions you have made in the course of your life. Which college should you attend? Should you marry this person? Can you answer God's call to ministry? How did you make those decisions? As she was writing this book, Lucy was preparing to celebrate her twenty-fifth wedding anniversary. This significant milestone gave her an opportunity to reflect upon the important decision that she made twenty-seven years ago when she and her husband began to talk about getting married. In those discussions that went on for hours, their feelings of love and respect were combined with more logical questions—are we compatible, do we have common goals—and out of this mixture of feeling and logic came the decision to marry.

This relationship between reason and emotion is an essential aspect of the human capacity to arrive at a judgment or an interpretation, for both reason and emotion are central to our humanity. A holistic view of human reason integrates the rational and the emotive. In fact, we need to be wary of those for whom this relationship is out of balance. Remember Mr. Spock of *Star Trek* fame? He epitomized the belief of the ancient Stoic philosophers who thought that feelings clouded and hindered rationality, that they must be denied in order for someone to reason well. Both of us have noticed that raising teenagers can be the opposite experience. Occasionally it seems like they can be all feeling and no judgment. Finding the balance is important. And finding it in preaching is important as well. But to do that we must overcome some misconceptions about emotions and feelings.

While we must be ready to recognize the intense power of feelings and the importance that they play in moving us to action, we must also be aware that we learn to develop control over our feelings. When we are children, and are angered by someone's actions, that intense feeling of anger is immediately demonstrated through our actions. We may show our anger by hitting or yelling at that person. Yet, when that person hits us back or our parents punish us, we begin to learn not to act on our feelings. We are not the victims of our emotions. Rather, our feelings and our intellect combine in creative and energizing ways to make us the people that we are. To be human is to be a thinking and a feeling person.

We asked you to think about important decisions in your life. Think about your decision to become a follower of Christ. You would be an unusual person if, after reading the Bible, purely on the basis of logical thought, you made the decision to become a

Christian. Does anyone become a Christian because it is "the log-ical thing to do?" We don't think so. We are not denying that there is a cognitive component to becoming a Christian. Rather, we are saying that *reason* itself is both rational and emotional.

Scripture is filled with stories of people's emotional responses to God's love. We have already noted that Luke tells of disciples whose hearts were burning within them as they listened to the res-urrected Jesus. Think of Thomas. In most of the Gospels he is just a name on a list. However, he comes alive on the pages of John's Gospel in his cryptic remarks in several stories. The first time is when the disciples are trying to convince Jesus it would be insane to go back to Judea regardless of how sick Lazarus is. They fail to convince him. So Thomas says "Let us also go, that we may die with him" (John 11:16). Now how would you inflect that? Triumphantly? Valiantly? Try saying it out loud. (Bob votes for cynically.) Then there's the Thomas who is deliriously relieved to hear Jesus announce he is about to leave and where he goes the disciples cannot follow. All Thomas hears is the language of a last minute escape plan. Only, he's confused about where to ren-dezvous: "Lord, we do not know where you are going. How can we know the way?" (John 14:5). Then there is the devastated Thomas, too emotionally numb even to have been hiding for fear of his own life, "Unless I see . . . I will not believe" (John 20:25). And finally, in the one moment to which the entire Gospel pre-sentation builds, there is the astonished Thomas who *gets* what the other disciples had yet to *understand*—who answers Jesus' loving invitation to believe by exclaiming "My Lord and my God!" (John 20:28). Should we ever try to figure out what part of that confession of faith is an emotional response and what part is rational?

Emotions and feelings are inextricably bound up with our belief because our life in faith is ultimately grounded in the love of God who calls forth faith from us. To preach the love and the forgive-ness of God and the good news of new life demands that we preach with a balance of reason and emotions. The emotions of the preacher and the emotions of the listeners must be brought into the service of this most important task.

It is the duty of the preacher to be attentive to and use these most powerful tools wisely and intentionally. Rhetorical theory assists us in doing that.

Pathos in Classical Rhetoric

Near the beginning of book 1, chapter 2 of the *Rhetoric,* Aristotle notes that it is not enough to look at how a speaker constructs an appropriate persona and how arguments are constructed. The speaker must also take responsibility "for disposing the listener in some way." This idea of disposing audience members in a particular way is what the classical notion of *pathos* is all about. The study of understanding how to bring about moods and feelings in listeners is necessary so that listeners may be roused and persuaded to make an appropriate response.[4] Therefore, according to classical rhetoric the question is not whether one should or should not use emotional appeals. Rather, it is a question of how and to what emotion or emotions one will appeal.

Where popular usage treats *pathos* as little more than a literate synonym for *pity, sentimentality,* or *suffering,* the rhetorical notion actually refers to the whole range of emotional reactions the audience experiences as affecting them. In this sense *pathos* involves not just my experience of an emotion but, through the experiencing of that emotion, the recognition that what the speaker is saying is affecting me. Through the arousal of certain feelings, I am being prepared to hear persuasive arguments that will encourage me to act.[5] This is why concern for *pathos* requires that a speaker consider all aspects of the listener's experience and what she or he brings to the rhetorical situation in the process of "disposing" them in a particular way. We will return to this later in the chapter.

We have already noted that popular thought has a tendency to cast rationality and emotion as two separate human capacities. Should we be surprised that Aristotle knew reason cannot be separated from emotion as if the latter is somehow an extrarational enchantment? He found that human passions are intimately related to judgment and that without drawing upon them, judgment is incomplete.[6] So rather than warning against making sentimental or manipulative appeals, he argued that good speakers are distinguished from manipulative ones by virtue of their moral purpose. He also argued that good speakers have a developed sense of ethics on how to make appropriate appeals. Regardless of how virtuous the purpose, virtuous ends do not justify improper means.

The human mind brings reason and feelings together to direct actions toward specific goals. It takes both reason and emotion to motivate someone. The word "emotion" is derived from the Latin verb *movere*, which means "to move." As indicated above, the ancients first reflected on "emotions" in an effort to understand how to *move* people to act through a speech. Because an emotion moves humans to do things, its role in motivation can be compared to the action of spark plugs in an automobile. Gasoline may enter a combustion chamber, but without the spark igniting the process nothing happens. Control of *pathos* is control of that spark. We have yet to fully understand the dynamic relationship between reason and emotion in humans, but without it our motivations would probably be reduced to little more than satisfying basic needs for food, shelter, and clothing. You may be tempted to add other drives like the sex drive to this list, but try to imagine a "drive" that does not require an emotional motivation.

Unlike arguments which can easily drift into abstractions (for example, sermonic explanations of doctrine or biblical teachings), emotions are active feelings we experience about someone or something. We readily identify emotions as feelings like anger, passion, pleasure, or pride. But such emotions are rarely, if ever, felt in the abstract. We feel emotions like these about someone or something. We love our spouse. We feel pride in our child's achievements. We experience euphoria when a long anticipated dream comes to fruition. Feelings attached to actual experiences are part of our judgments concerning those people and events.[7] The most effective use of emotion in a speech occurs when it helps listeners understand why you, as the speaker, *care* in a way that helps them, as listeners, *care* as well. This is why we can say that implicit to responding actively to the arguments of any persuasive effort is knowing why the speaker *cares*. Whether by intention or default, things we say in the sermon will evoke an emotional response from our listeners. We believe it is important for preachers to understand the factors that help make listeners receptive to the persuasive goal of a sermon's emotional appeal.

DEVELOPING THE EMOTIONAL APPEAL OF A SERMON

No one enters the sanctuary as a blank slate. People bring to their worship of God and engagement with the Word of God the content and confusion, anger and joy, as well as the peace and sorrows of their lives. They also bring their own faith with its questions and convictions. To this our liturgies add the hymns, anthems, readings, and even the expressions of congregational life that are all part of worship meant to arouse emotional and thoughtful responses. Somewhere in this mix falls the sermon, one of a number of elements that affects the feelings or emotional disposition of listeners. So as we look at what is involved in crafting the shape of the emotional appeal, we need to keep this context in view. When preaching, you can, and should, attempt to affect the emotional response of your listeners. You want them to care about what you have to say or why speak? Nevertheless, what happens in the sermon is only part of what goes into shaping the response of listeners. Any effort to have the sermon control more than this is where controlling the means of persuasion becomes manipulative and unethical.

There are also a variety of ways we develop the emotional tone of our sermons. Many of these are related to style and delivery. For example, the tone of voice we use, our facial expressions, and our body language all convey our passion and involvement with our message. Our choice of words, as well as the images, illustrations, and examples that we use, may please or irritate. We will discuss some of these concerns when we take up the subject of style in chapter 7. In this chapter we have chosen to examine the two most significant dimensions involved in developing a rhetorical stance with regard to how *pathos* creates the emotional appeal of a sermon. The first of these is discovering how to create presence through identification. The second is making sure there is a real connection between the audience a sermon assumes and the audience that is actually listening to the sermon.

Creating Presence: The Imagination of the Heart

One of the most frustrating phrases we can hear is "I don't care." When we care very deeply about some issue we are cut to the quick when someone looks us in the eye and tells us that she "couldn't care less." There may be a variety of reasons that she does not care. She may be too busy or too lazy, too preoccupied or too selfish, too indifferent, or too afraid. The reason for her response may not be clear, but what is clear is that before we can ask her to make a decision or to act, she must be brought to care. So the question we face as we begin to think about a sermon must be "How will she come to care?"

One way rhetoricians and homileticians have identified to help make this happen comes about as the speaker or preacher gains control of the imaginative ability to create presence for bringing a matter before the consciousness of listeners. Kenneth Burke reminds us:

> Aristotle had said that, particularly in arousing pity, the rhetorician is most effective if he can bring before the audience the actual evidence of hardship and injustice suffered. Thus, in proportion as "imagination" went up in the scale of motivational values, one can speak of an appeal to the *imagination* in many instances which classical theory might have treated as persuasion by the appeals of *pathos* and *ethos*....In sum, today any representation of passions, emotion, actions, and even mood and personality, is likely to be treated as falling under the heading of "images," which in turn explicitly involve "imagination."[8]

So making use of images and imagination are significant factors in helping people to care by creating presence for the question or concern at stake in that identification. In this sense, imaginative use of images, examples, and illustrations need to serve the ongoing task of creating this *presence*.

Ancient rhetoricians like Aristotle described this as the process of "bringing-before-the-eyes" (*Rhetoric* 3.10-11). A Chinese aphorism embodies this idea: "A king sees an ox on its way to sacrifice. He is moved to pity for it and orders that a sheep be used in its place. He confesses he did so because he could see the ox, but not the sheep."[9] Listeners care about that which is made present to them, suggesting that dwelling on a subject by way of a variety of rhetorical techniques is the way a speaker can create the desired emotions in the consciousness of listeners. The less immediate the concern or the more distant in time or place, the greater the need to be able to create presence if we want listeners to care.[10]

This ancient concept of creating presence as a way to get listeners to care is often discussed as the process of creating *identification*. During the past quarter century many homiletical theorists have adopted Burke's redefinition of persuasion as the art of creating identification.[11] Burke argued that identification functions as an appeal in three ways:

Persuasion by association: the most simple level, in which a communicator attempts to sway listeners by announcing ways in which they hold common cause.
Persuasion by dissociation: a more complex level, which focuses on ways division can sharpen the possibility of unity. Otherwise disparate groups or opposed individuals can be persuaded to make common cause by this strategy of creating identification.
Persuasion by creating presence: the most sophisticated level, in which the listener is unaware of the ways in which the identification has been forged.[12]

Notice that the last of these three has more to do with *pathos* than *logos*. It is persuasion that comes by way of indirection through images and connections the speaker makes with the listener. Once identification gets forged, Burke says, listeners tend to *unconsciously* persuade themselves.

Recent preaching theory has placed a great deal of emphasis on these three forms of creating identification. For example, Buttrick has argued that a Christian rhetoric has three *intentions:* associating, dissociating, and connecting everyday life with "convictional understanding" of faith by a "bringing into view our unspoken faith" through "a bringing out through language."[13] Since the latter is largely accomplished with the same tools Aristotle suggested as useful in "bringing-before-the-eyes"—depiction, analogy, and metaphor—it is clear that Buttrick views it as a form of what we are describing as the task of *creating presence.* Thus, Buttrick concludes that "Preaching does not persuade in the sense of arguing the truth of the gospel; preaching sets the gospel in lived experience, genuine experience, so that truth will be acknowledged."[14] In whichever of its three intentions, this is persuasion as the art of creating identification. *Pathos,* more than *logos* or *ethos,* is the means of persuasion that is most concerned with understanding how to *move* the audience into caring about and then acting on what is said. We stated above that if a speaker wants listeners to care, listeners need to be able to hear why the speaker cares. But making sure your passion and concern for what is being discussed is appropriately constructed and credibly conveyed is an aspect of *ethos.* It is a projection of the speaker's character or *persona.* Your passion is part of who you are in the moment of preaching. You must not only care about what you are saying, but you must also demonstrate your concern so that you will involve your listeners and get them to care as well.

As we noted in the previous chapter on *ethos,* it is important that listeners trust and feel connected with the speaker. Therefore, when we use words and patterns of speech that are familiar, gestures that connect, and recognizable images, we are identifying with our listeners and they, almost unconsciously, are identifying with us. In turn, by listening to our audience, hearing their joys and concerns, questions, and pains, as well as the ways that they express themselves, we begin to move into a much deeper relationship with them. Through our preaching we are able to address their needs. We recognize the importance of this kind of identification when we realize how uncomfortable we are writing a sermon for a congregation that we do not know and with whom we have never worshiped. When we "drop in" as the visiting preacher it is much more difficult to use images and illustrations that have a sense of immediacy. Therefore, an equally important dimension of *pathos* is getting to know the congregation.

Connecting with the Congregation

Who are *they?* For most preachers an audience is often an ill-defined, hazy conception even when a particular congregation may be in view. It is ill defined because we tend to treat an audience impersonally as if it is a "thing" out there. We develop a generalized image of the potential listeners and let it supply the totality of our assumptions about the context. More than turning "audience" into an abstraction, it actually turns our conception of an audience into a metaphor.[15] We *fictionalize* a conception of the congregation and then cast them in this metaphorical role in the process of developing the sermon. As obvious as it may be on reflection, we need to remind ourselves that the listeners we conceive while composing a sermon are not the same thing as the people who eventually listen to it. Unless a sermon is being composed in a wholly extemporaneous fashion, our conception of a sermon's audience is actually a kind of fabrication.[16]

Consider a specific preaching circumstance, one with a particularly narrow conception of the audience defined by an appropriate response.[17] Imagine a child of the congregation you pastor suddenly and tragically dies. The urgency to this situation is magnified by the unfinished sense of this life. The people that gather know and love the child and they look to you for some kind of appropriate response. Of course, the difficulty of framing an appropriate response is to navigate between a completely deficient response (for example, "God needed her more than we did") and one that helplessly concedes despair (for example, "All we can do is mourn this loss"). Even in the specificity of this urgent situation, with its known audience, and its clearly defined constraints, we would say that during the process of composing what you hope is an appropriate sermon, there will still be a difference between the audience you assume and the actual audience who will gather to listen to what you have prepared to say. The reason we make this claim is because rhetoricians make a distinction between the concrete audience that listens to a speech and the audience the speech constructs by its assumptions about the listeners. The former is outside the text, while the latter is inside. More often than not the difference between these two conceptions is at the heart of the problem when we come away from a worship service somehow feeling as if the sermon we preached or the sermon we heard never really "connected." The failed connection is usually a disparity between the response of the audience we imagined being moved by the sermon and the response of the audience that actually listened to it.

Generic sermons make for a bland diet, indeed. No wonder a sustained ministry of such sermons deserves the sobriquet that it serves up "salt-free Christianity." One-size-fits-all sermons conjure images of congregations who long for what Richard Weaver has called "the spaciousness of old rhetoric." This was a phrase he used to describe the lofty quality of much nineteenth-century oratory which was composed with the assumption that listeners shared a common morality and a common cultural identity.[18] We will explore the appeal of this style of preaching at greater length in chapter 7. Here we simply state that it was an inaccurate cultural conception then and, as a way of thinking about preaching in our pluralistic culture, it would be disastrous today. The Gospel must be tailored to situations and to specific groups of listeners. And we think this is what the Bible suggests as well. From the very outset of the Christian story it became apparent that there could not be *one* sermon. Of course it would save a great deal of time, energy, and anguish if each Sunday morning you could get up in the pulpit and deliver the same sermon over again. Busy pastors are occasionally tempted to subscribe to homiletic resources and just preach the sermons that come in the mail. Or, if it was a matter of picking the appropriate text that addresses a specific congregational need, basic sermons could be packaged in some contemporary version of *The Expositors Dictionary of Texts* or in lectionary resources with one master sermon developed from the "theme" of each text.[19] This would mean that preachers would be able to spend their time becoming masters of deft delivery rather than sweating through the processes of exegesis and sermon crafting. And the *too* busy pastor responds, "Wouldn't that be nice?"

You might note that we have come dangerously close to meddling at this point. We all know that there is no end of the generic sermon sources that can become like an addiction in the face of ever diminishing time to prepare. Thankfully, the church recognized early on that each group of hearers and each situation is different. Congregations need sermons constructed just for them. Lenora Tubbs Tisdale argues, preachers need to become as sophisticated in *exegeting congregations* as they are in exegeting texts.[20] She has turned the public speaking dictum "Know your audience" into an important call for preachers to identify the worldviews, values, and character of a congregation and localize the gospel to this context. We know that good authors are adept at listening to the people around them, listening to their culture, and identifying contexts that speak to the human condition. Preachers are called to the same task by becoming exegetes of their cultural contexts. The experience of the early church bears witness to this. Look at the audience for Peter's Pentecost sermon in Acts 2:5-8:

> Now there were devout Jews from every nation under heaven living in Jerusalem. And at this sound the crowd gathered and was bewildered, because each one heard them speaking in the native language of each. Amazed and astonished, they asked, "Are not these who are speaking Galileans? And how is it that we hear, each of us, in our own native language?"

The gift of the Spirit given at Pentecost was the ability to shape words so that each listener heard the message clearly in his or her own native language. There is a rhetorical lesson here for all preachers. The gospel may be universal, but it must be presented in a way that can be heard by the real audience that shows up to listen. This kind of preaching comes from knowing the congregation. And this kind of knowing can only come through listening.

Too often preachers think of themselves as the individual who is supposed to have an appropriate word to say for all occasions.

However, listening may be the more essential quality of effective pastoral ministry. Parishioners generally value ministers more for their ability to listen empathetically than for the ability to have the right answer or for an ability to say something that will "fix" whatever the presenting problem may be. Learning how to cultivate interpersonal communication skills of both *empathetic* and *dialogic* listening all week long are required ethnographic tools for the preacher who wants to preach sermons that will connect with the actual audience who comes to listen on Sunday.

We make use of *empathetic* listening skills when we learn how to focus closely on the perspective of the other one speaking. Many people are inclined to fill the silences in conversation with a rush of their own words rather than trying to draw out their conversation partners. Learning to listen to the congregation requires the preacher to solicit the perceptions of parishioners and then listen as they share them. It requires being *with* people.

In those times when listening needs to be more than empathetic, preachers can make use of *dialogic* listening skills. Instead of "making our points" or "getting my side across" in the conversation, we listen and converse by engaging in a process of "collaborative" meaning making. Both kinds of listening will change our preaching. Listeners will discover both themselves and ideas they helped create in what we say in the sermon.[21] But there is another kind of listening that is required of preachers who would know their audience. Preachers must engage in a particular kind of reflective listening that questions the existing assumptions of the larger culture and brings the gospel to bear on the differences. As we were writing this chapter Bob monitored a fascinating debate between a speaker and a listener in his public speaking course. In her speech, the speaker offered the standard value argument that the death penalty serves as a deterrent against capital crime. But during the question and answer session, a classmate challenged, "Hey, I don't know what suburb you're living in, but guys I know who live to mix it up go 'Live hard. Live fast. Leave a pretty corpse.' Don't you get it? Death penalties only scare people who want to get married and grow old. They don't scare guys who actually plan on dying young."

Imagine having a question and answer session after a sermon where listeners challenge us: "Do *you* know what *you're* talking about?" Imagine that. In fact, we need to imagine that! Only, we need to imagine it before we preach. For sermons to speak the Word of God, preachers must become adept at exegeting the pre-suppositions of culture. This means that the preacher has to go one step further than simply being an astute observer. The preacher has to bring the gospel to bear on the inadequate worldviews that give rise to both arguments put forward by the students in the example above. It is not enough to be ahead of the game. The preacher needs to have faithfully exegeted the congregation, faithfully exegeted contemporary culture, and faithfully allowed the radical Word of the gospel to provide the lens through which he or she and the congregation understand their identity as the people of God for their time and their cultural context. Only then can the preacher speak the Word of hope.

FURTHERING THE CONVERSATION

For some preachers the idea of preaching a sermon without strong emotional appeal and passionate delivery is inconceivable, while others are quite suspicious of any preaching that depends upon a strong emotional response from the preacher or the listeners. Lucy teaches at a seminary that includes students from a wide variety of denominations. They have some very lively discussions in the preaching *practica,* for example, when African Methodist Episcopal students critique Presbyterians and vice versa. Each denomination has very different ideas of the role and quality of *pathos* in the sermon. Students who have not had a great deal of experience listening to sermons outside of their home churches find that they must learn how to listen to these new approaches. The students learn that all sermons have an emotional tone and appeal, but some must learn how to develop control over their emotions, while others have to learn that, as David Buttrick observes, it is "emphatically unnatural" to subdue our emotions and use an understated, modulated tone when we are preaching such good news.[22]

With the growing interest in developing contemporary styles of worship and preaching, the emotional tone of the sermon and the passion of the preacher are of increasing concern. Many are coming to recognize the importance of emotion in establishing and maintaining interest. However, while searching for ways to make their preaching "come alive," some preachers confuse an emotional, enthusiastic delivery style and the absence of a manuscript or notes with a sermon that takes *pathos* seriously. We disagree. Stirring up the emotions of the congregations, whether in holy joy or righteous indignation, without serious attention to *ethos* and *logos* should frustrate listeners. We wish we could say "will frustrate," but one need not look far to find too many listeners who are willing to confuse enthusiasm with the Holy Spirit. A constructive theology of preaching requires a rhetorical stance that balances *pathos* with *ethos* and *logos*, creating sermons that move rather than manipulate. *Pathos* prepares the listeners, but it is not an end in itself. It tills the soil of our hearts and minds and gets us ready, but the arguments, the challenge of the gospel, and the call to follow the risen Christ, who has set all our hearts on fire, must follow.

On Creating Presence by Imaging Ideas

Homileticians have begun to recognize the importance of the use of images and imagination as a way of creating presence for what is at stake in a sermon. Emotion and feeling are not to be avoided. Rather, they are to be nurtured and cultivated. For only by connecting with our congregations, in both their heads and their hearts, will our preaching connect.

Some of the most sage advice budding novelists must learn is, "Don't explain it. Show it." This is advice preachers would do well to heed. How often does your mind wander when a speaker goes into the stratosphere of abstraction. To get a sense of what we mean, take the following abstraction test. Look through several of your sermons and try to determine what percentage of your presentation is dedicated to explaining abstractions or ideas and what portion is dedicated to the kind of showing that trusts itself to creating an image or an experience that does not have to be explained. In other words, illustrations that you use to "drive home a point" don't count. Novelists do not explain what they have shown. They trust readers to get it without color commentary. They create an experience of meaning readers go through. What it meant to the reader is finally up to the reader and not the novelist. So how much of your sermon is abstracted and illustrated *explanation* and how much is *imaged* experience where you trust the listeners to "get it"?

• QUESTIONS FOR GROUP DISCUSSION

Using a sermon you have analyzed in advance, discuss with one another how the preacher has used image and imagination in the development of an issue at stake. How does the preacher bring the issue before your eyes and involve you in it? How does the preacher use emotions and feelings to get you to care? Are there moments in which the preacher shows it rather than explains it? Was the preacher right to trust the listener in such moments?

On Creating Appropriate Pathos Versus Manipulation

Of the three means of persuasion *pathos* is most open to blatant manipulation. Without a balanced interest in *logos* and *ethos*, *pathos* can easily slide into a dangerous preoccupation of creating effect for effect's sake. Exercised in balance with the other means of persuasion, it is an essential aspect of effective communication. *Pathos* is also the means most closely associated with "identification." In this chapter we have noted that many homileticians would readily accept Burke's redefinition of rhetoric as an art of "creating identification." Moving listeners to care is essential and they respond to the fact that you care and that you are someone with whom they can identify and trust.

• QUESTIONS FOR GROUP DISCUSSION

Where should the line be drawn concerning ethically acceptable ways of creating identification and ethically manipulative efforts? Review some of your recent sermons. What did you use to create identification between you and your listeners? Why did you include such information about yourself or commonly held ideas and opinions? How did they contribute to the goal of the sermon? Use one sermon for group discussion.

On Listening to Our Listeners

Learning to exegete the cultural context is only the first step in learning how to write a sermon in which our listeners can find themselves. Looking back over existing sermons, most preachers quickly realize which sermons were written for a particular group at a particular time, and which ones are "evergreens," which are sermons capable of being preached in multiple contexts. "Evergreen" sermons tend to construct a general, universal audience, as opposed to the sermon that is defined by the rhetorical situation. One addresses a universal audience with concerns relevant to being alive at this time and in this culture. The other sermon addresses an audience attuned to the specific realities of a particular presenting problem, or what a congregation or community may need to hear at any given time.

Lucy has noted over the years that one of the challenges for those moving from the seminary to the congregation is the move from universal to more contextual sermons. She helps her students from the very beginning by having them write sermons for a specific worshiping community, whether they will actually preach them there or not. On the other hand, Bob (the rhetorician as true believer) is uncomfortable having listeners imagine they are someone else when they hear a fellow student speak. He is a stickler on the subject that "constructed" audiences must be real. He has students turn in a written sermon composed for their own worshiping community. Either way, the point is that preachers must learn to contextualize sermons. Having a few "evergreen" sermons in the portfolio is valuable. Learning to contextualize preaching for specific audiences is essential. If a new preaching opportunity arises and you look back over an old sermon only to discover that you can't possible preach it to this group of people, then you are on the right track.

• QUESTIONS FOR GROUP DISCUSSION

Using the text of a preacher whose craft you admire, analyze the way in which the individual has shaped the sermon for her or his listeners. What understandings of the immediate or the larger cultural context helped the preacher bring listeners to a moment of individual or collective discovery or insight? How has the preacher written this sermon for the particular community?

READ MORE ABOUT IT

David Buttrick. "Developing Moves" in *Homiletic: Moves and Structures*. Philadelphia: Fortress Press, 1987.

Craig Loscalzo. *Preaching Sermons that Connect: Effective Communication Through Identification*. Downers Grove, Ill.: InterVarsity Press, 1992.

John S. McClure. *The Roundtable Pulpit: Where Leadership & Preaching Meet*. Nashville: Abingdon Press, 1995.

Nora Tubbs Tisdale. *Preaching as Local Theology and Folk Art*. Minneapolis: Fortress Press, 1997.

Chapter 5

What Am I Going to Say?

What, then, is an argument? From the perspective of communication, rhetorically, anything we experience, anything we see or hear, do or read, or think about, or say, can be interpreted in a great many ways, each of which is an argument; that is, a structure of communication is an argument, and it is arguments that convey meaning.

—Zahava Karl McKeon, *Novels and Arguments: Inventing Rhetorical Criticism*[1]

In the beginning was the Word, and the Word was with God, and the Word was God.

—John 1:1

IN THE BEGINNING WAS THE LOGOS

A HUMBLED COLLEAGUE recently confessed to Lucy, "I was all set to preach a sermon this Sunday until I actually thought about who I was going to be preaching to." An emergency had arisen in a nearby congregation and this person happily accepted the hurried request to preach in the pastor's absence. He was looking forward to the opportunity both to help a friend and visit a different congregation. So there was no hesitation in accepting the invitation. Besides, he had initially decided, he could use *that* sermon he had recently preached for his home congregation.

He quickly informed the church secretary of his title and text. Then, as Sunday drew nearer, he printed out the sermon to review and rehearse it. The sermon, based on Luke 18:18, explored the story of the rich young man. It ended with a call to rethink the importance of wealth and material possessions based on Jesus'

89

call to surrender the hold we have on possessions and the hold they have on us. The original audience for the sermon consisted of parishioners in an affluent suburban congregation; people who, with a little help, had no trouble recognizing themselves in the rich young ruler. Lucy's colleague had constructed the sermon in a way that the parishioners, who made the connection with the rich young man of the biblical text, could hear, not only Jesus' judgment, but Jesus' promise and invitation to an alternative life full of possibilities. He chose to use a strategy of indirection rather than confrontation in creating the identification. When the sermon was finished, he knew it had worked. Instead of the "nice sermon" pleasantries in the greeting line, people were stopping to engage him with thoughtful questions and remarks. Several members of the congregation admitted it would be scary but refreshing to rethink their settled issues of status and security.

As Lucy's colleague recalled how well that sermon had connected, he reread it with an eye for how it might connect with Sunday's congregation. Suddenly he realized he would have to compose something quite different. The sermon did not ring true for an inner-city congregation whose members were struggling with unemployment and underemployment—people well beyond the margins of affluence. How would they hear a call to give up all that they had when most of them had very little? With only a few days left he began to rework the sermon. Relative to the concept we discussed in chapter 4, he was "learning to listen" to this new audience. So, having envisioned a very different congregation, he returned and read the passage in Luke again, looked again at the commentaries, and prayerfully reflected on how this story could speak God's word to a people many of whom would like to be faced with the rich young man's dilemma. What was God's word for this people? And who was he to call them to discover it? All those good reasons in his first sermon no longer worked. And to his surprise he discovered that even the best of reasons are often very contextual.

Having discussed the character of the speaker and the passion of the listeners, issues that we are usually willing to concede are contextual, one would think that a discussion of arguments, *logos*, would finally get down to eternal, immutable, fixed truths—the content of the sermon. However, as Lucy's friend discovered, this rarely, if ever, is the situation. In his book *Faithful Persuasion*, theologian David Cunningham asks a crucial question, "Can the arguments themselves really be identified in the abstract? Can they even *exist* apart from their specific rhetorical contexts?"[2] Rhetoric, therefore, is all about helping the speaker, or preacher in this case, respect the power of words, the contextual and situational nature of arguments, and the dynamic character of persuasion.

In this chapter we turn our attention to the final of Aristotle's three means of persuasion—*logos*. This is the words, the content, our good reasons, what we *say* in our sermon. When we focus on *logos*, we look not only at the creative power of the words, but also at the importance of choosing those words carefully. *Logos*, in rhetoric, is concerned with actively thinking about and reflecting on the situation, and then making appropriate choices of words and arguments given the situation, the listeners, and God's call to bold proclamation. Through an examination of the classical understanding of *logos* and argumentation, we use this chapter to explore the contextual nature of arguments as good reasons, the basic structures of an argument, and the sources of where we find arguments. The real questions many a preacher has asked at one time or another are: "How do I figure out what I am going to say? Is there some way to get kick started when you stare at the empty screen on your computer? And what counts as good reasons for believing something, anyway?"

A Good Person Offering Good Reasons to Good People

Puffery, manipulation, mere rhetoric, empty rhetoric, false and misleading rhetoric—every epithet imaginable has been lobbed at rhetoric over the millennia. Certainly some speakers, in their efforts to achieve their ends no matter what, have been utterly Machiavellian in their use of the art of rhetoric.[3] But that is not what we, nor any ethical rhetoric teacher, would suggest. At the same time, we are also aware that there is enough history here that to even raise the question of argument's relationship to preaching is to step into a hotly debated minefield between rhetoric and homiletics. Or, as one friend calls it, a question that's "all mines and no field." Nevertheless, it is a field all of us enter every day, every time we engage anyone else in conversation. As any communication theorist will remind us, as soon as we engage another in conversation we enter into the process of persuasion.

If you recall our discussion of the tensive relationship between preaching and rhetoric in chapter 2, you will recall that it is around the issues of truth and persuasive argument, namely *logos*, that homiletics felt that it was necessary to renounce rhetoric. We will not rehearse that argument here, but as we enter into the discussion of persuasion and argument it is important to clarify what we mean by *argument*. Consider Zahava Karl McKeon's definition in the epigraph of this chapter. According to this definition, arguments are at the center of our efforts to convey meaning to one another. When considered in this way, McKeon finds that even stoplights are an argument—one that most of us who drive internalized some time ago. But if you doubt that they are an argument, just think back to the last time that you came to an utterly deserted intersection at 2:00 A.M. and the light had just turned red. There is not a soul or a sound for blocks. Do you wait? The point is, even if the question is only briefly entertained before being dismissed, it still means that the old, previously resolved, internal debate has suddenly reemerged.

We suggest that much of the rejection of persuasion and argument is based on faulty definitions. For example, some people, including some contemporary homileticians, view all persuasion as manipulation or coercion.[4] Still others view argument as synonymous with disagreement or quarrel, signaling a breakdown in communication and relationship. But, if an argument is virtually any structure of communication that attempts to create meaning for a listener, then argument is an integral aspect of preaching. And so is persuasion. Whether we are trying to convince our child of the importance of doing homework (certainly all "mine" and no "field") or preaching to our congregation on a Sunday morning, we have a point of view, and we offer reasons we hope our listeners will find convincing and compelling. Even though some preachers want to avoid even the appearance that they are trying to persuade listeners while preaching, it is almost impossible for humans to speak without expressing a point of view we hope others will come to share. Therefore, repudiating the role of persuasion in preaching may be less helpful than acknowledging and then finding ways to value different points of view in our sermons. The real question may have more to do with how overt versus how collaborative our approach to persuasion will be, since the role of persuasion in preaching is always one of degree, rather than kind.[5]

The Rhetorical Occasion: When Facts Are Not Enough

What makes argument so challenging is that *logos*, or our good reasons, are needed whenever the *facts* will not speak for themselves. Each year, for example, most clergy find it necessary to address the issue of stewardship in a sermon. It is one of those facts we wish *would* speak for itself, but many parishioners need a little help to understand how giving translates into ministry possibilities. Most preachers try to stress the importance of stewardship as our response to God's gracious gift of life. At the same time, they also have to find ways to convey the "fact" that financial support of the church is crucial to its continued existence as a functioning organization. How do we go about choosing the arguments and reasons that will persuade people to give to God and to the church?

A central point in our stewardship sermon may be a call to ask parishioners to help repair the church roof. We know that repairing the roof will cost $10,000. That sum is a fact. The proof of that fact is supplied by the signed estimate from the roofing company. While speaking to the congregation, we can actually hold the estimate in hand, look at it, and cite the bottom-line figure of $10,000. However, once we make the move toward trying to convince parishioners to contribute money for the repair, we have ventured into a realm that requires rhetoric. We may offer a variety of reasons to encourage them to pledge funds. For their part, though they try to support the congregation, they still have to decide whether this appeal is something to which they would be willing to respond at this time. As preachers, we are free to offer parishioners our good reasons for giving, and parishioners, in turn, are free to decide whether or not to accept those good reasons as motivations to act.

So using rhetoric becomes necessary whenever we offer our opinion, or make a case for choosing one option from several possibilities. Whenever the generally agreed upon facts are not enough, whenever there are a variety of possible responses or actions, whenever people of good faith and good intentions still disagree about the outcome, rhetoric is necessary. If you think about it, that makes rhetoric necessary for most of the communication in our life.

Rhetoric relies on a good person offering good reasons. You may recall from chapter 2 that Quintilian defined oratory as a "good man speaking well." Historically, rhetoric has defined a good person as one who respects and honors the listener and has the best interest of the listener in mind. Our concept of "ethics" is derived from this aspect of *ethos* we discussed in chapter 3. But what of "good reasons"? By *good* do we mean truthful? Is a good reason the best reason the speaker can discern? The challenge in thinking rhetorically is to sift through all of the good reasons and discern which of those reasons the listener will find persuasive. Good rhetorical reasons, therefore, are reasons that are both truthful and compelling and convincing to the listener.

In our stewardship sermon, as we try to persuade parishioners to contribute to the church, we might argue that they should donate money to the church because, "Where your treasure is, there will your heart be also." Another good reason would be the importance of stewardship in supporting the church and its mission. However, the reason one whole group of parishioners might find most compelling is that the leak is directly over the pew in which they customarily sit. While that may not be the most "biblical" argument or the loftiest appeal, there is no getting around the fact that it is a compelling argument either to move or to help pay to have the roof fixed.

When we make a claim, offer a proposal, state a proposition, or suggest an opinion, and then invite others to join us in agreeing with it and acting on it, we are making an argument. We then offer evidence, reasons, and data to assist our listeners in making a judgment as to whether or not they will accept our claim. A description of what is involved in making argument in this manner is a central part of Aristotle's *Rhetoric*. After defining the kind of persuasion that comes through character *(ethos)* and the kind of persuasion that occurs because listeners are led to feel emotion *(pathos),* Aristotle says of the third means of persuasion, "Persuasion [also] occurs through arguments *[logoi]* when we show the truth or the apparent truth from whatever is persuasive in each case" (1.2.6). Good speakers shape how listeners view them as speakers *(ethos),* involve listeners emotionally *(pathos),* and shape the reasons offered by sifting though the possible arguments, making choices about what to include and what to exclude *(logos).* This is why Aristotle maintained that persuading others depends on making appeals based on who we are, on making appeals to their passion and aspirations, and on making appeals through arguments grounded in practical reasoning.

Phronesis: Practical Reason

Central to Aristotle's understanding of rhetorical argument was the distinction between *epistêmê* and *phronêsis*. *Epistêmê* is formal logic that is undisputed, universal, and eternally true and applicable in all situations. It is the kind of reasoning philosophers use in formal logic. *Phronêsis*, on the other hand, is the logic or reasoning of the orator. *Phronêsis* is about *practical* reasoning. Though still rationally based, phronêsis takes into account the concrete situation and attempts to apply reasons to a specific situation and a specific audience urging a particular action or response. *Phronesis* (practical reasoning) is always concerned with application; *epistêmê* (logical reasoning) is not. *Phronêsis* is grounded in the communal and recognizes that not all truths are universal. Instead of trying to determine ultimate truths, *practical reasoning* is rhetorical reasoning, satisfied if it can gain agreement. This is why Aristotle is willing to acknowledge that persuasion can occur by way of "apparent truth."

Aristotle spends a good deal of time trying to show how rhetorical argument is like logical argument. In formal logic, one argues by offering first a major premise, then a minor premise, which, if both are accepted, leads logically to a "valid" conclusion. The classic post-Aristotelian example here (sexist language and all) is:

> If all men are mortal (major premise),
> and Socrates is a man (minor premise),
> then Socrates is mortal (conclusion).

In showing how a rhetorical argument emulates this form, Aristotle notes that everyday rhetorical reasoning simply leaves out one of the premises. He offers the following example:

> Dionysius is plotting to become a tyrant (conclusion)
> because he has recently instituted a personal guard (minor
> premise).[6]

The unspoken major premise of this kind of argument is: "Rulers who would be tyrants always form a personal guard first." However, listeners are probably far more concerned about Dionysius's alarming behavior than thinking about what has been left unsaid.

We could turn a logical argument into a rhetorical argument by letting the audience supply the apparent part of the argument. We might say, "Everybody is mortal, so Socrates is mortal." No one has to verbally add "Socrates is a person." We just intuitively supply the missing piece of the argument and, in the process, we join ourselves to the argument. In prepsychological language, Aristotle is making a connection that contemporary rhetoricians call, "creating *identification* with what the speaker is saying." When we intuitively supply part of the argument, it becomes a way of participating in the creation of the argument, a way for the speaker to sweep us up in what is being said.

Open your Bible to any letter of Paul's and you will have no trouble finding many rhetorical arguments. The fifth chapter of Romans opens with one: "Therefore, since we are justified by faith, we have peace with God through our Lord Jesus Christ."

(Rom. 5:1). The major premise is that people, who are justified through Jesus Christ, by faith, have peace with God. The minor premise is that we have been justified by faith. The conclusion, therefore, is that we have peace with God. Notice that Paul leaves out the major premise. He assumes that we will fill in the missing premise, which we do in a manner that invites our participation in the conclusion. The point is that most arguments are constructed in this rhetorical fashion rather than the full, syllogistic fashion. Rhetorical arguments have an unstated premise (usually the major premise) that speaker and listener alike must assume if the argument is to be accepted.

The Heart of the Matter: Warrants

The rhetorical argument (Aristotle called these *enthymemes*) depends totally on the involvement of the listeners and their assent to the premises of the speaker. But this can be tricky. There are times when no one (neither the speaker nor the listeners) are aware of the assumptions or premises held by each other. So before we look at the ways rhetoric offers to help us discover and discern what counts as "good reasons," we think it is important to look at a modern approach to understanding the structure of rhetorical arguments.

In the late 1950s the British philosopher, Stephen Toulmin, expanded and amplified Aristotle's approach in his book, *The Uses of Argument*. Toulmin sought to describe what he labeled as our everyday "working logic." We make arguments and claims in the court, in the academy, and in the pulpit that are far from pure logic. Since most arguments make use of practical reasoning rather than formal reasoning, he wanted to help people come up with a way to break down the parts of everyday argument. Not all arguments are born equal. So Toulmin developed a working logic to explore the way we "assess the soundness, strength and conclusiveness of arguments" in an everyday communal context.

Central to Toulmin's approach is the understanding of the "layout" or "physiological structure" of arguments. When we argue we present a claim (C). That claim is supported by data (D) and backed by warrants (W). If we want to look at it visually it would be:

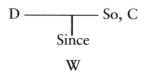

This may not seem very revolutionary, but what Toulmin helped us to understand was that the movement from data to claim is dependent upon warrants. Warrants answer the question, "how did you get from D to C?" Warrants are the underlying support, the justification for allowing certain data to support a certain claim. What is crucial, according to Toulmin, is that, while data are always explicit, warrants are usually implicit.[7] Discovering and/or being attentive to the warrants in our arguments is crucial, because, according to Toulmin, this is often the very point at which we disagree with a speaker or, as the speaker, we lose our listeners. Because warrants are often implicit (supplied by listeners), speakers may be completely unaware of the reason(s) why listeners reject a claim.

An example may help make this clearer. Let's go back to our stewardship sermon and think about how an implicit warrant may support our claim. What if, in our sermon, we raise the issue of the estimate for the roof repair as data in support of the claim that giving is needed. Perhaps we even hold up the estimate or project an image of it on an overhead screen. Our warrant for drawing attention to the estimate might be our assumption that members should take responsibility for debts incurred in the maintenance of the facility. But, what if some members of the congregation do not share that warrant. What if they are repelled by the use of such "data" as support for a claim in a *sermon*? At that point we have lost, or even angered, many of our listeners.

So let's say we decide to make the claim that people "should contribute to the church." Then we support this claim by using the biblical story of the grateful leper in Luke 17:11-19 as our data. We tell the story in a way that allows us to draw a conclusion concerning the importance of returning to God and giving thanks for what God has done for us. At this point we declare that responsible stewardship is one of the ways that, as church members, we can "return and give thanks." Telling the story, then, is the explicit support, or data, for our claim that Christians "should contribute to the church." Of course, there is still an implicit warrant, or what Toumlin calls "backing," in making this kind of claim. As preachers we assume (our warrant) that scripture helps us understand how to live the Christian life. Therefore, it is appropriate to appeal to scripture when making claims about how we are to live. Here we are assuming that our listeners believe scripture is an appropriate backing for support of our claim—an assumption preachers often make and most listeners accept. But we are also assuming (another warrant) that listeners equate maintaining church facilities with responsible ways to use money in expressing thanks to God. What if, rather than fixing leaks in buildings, some of our listeners believe good stewardship is better served by giving their money to the modern equivalent of people who have been healed and want to go back and help other "lepers." Here, even if listeners accept the first warrant (that scripture helps us to understand how to live), they may still reject the claim because of the second warrant (that roof repairs represent good ways to "return and give thanks").

Toulmin's way of breaking down the explicit and implicit components of an argument helps us to see that an important part of coming up with good reasons is somewhat like being a surgeon or archaeologist. We cannot assume that arguments which would persuade us will necessarily persuade the majority of our listeners. We need to open up our arguments, press behind them to think about what assumptions they bring to the table, and decide whether we believe our listeners will find those assumptions as compelling as we do. This kind of thinking forces preachers to get at the heart of the matter, and, often, it is at the heart of the matter that we are able to name the real obstacles to be overcome if our good reasons are to connect with our congregations.

Logos as a Rhetorical Stance

Logos helps us to understand that our speaking is always situated in a context, that is, it has a *Sitz im Leben*, a setting in life. When we begin to think about developing a message or argument, we must consider the situation, identify the central or crucial question or issues. We must then review and collect all of the available supporting materials, such as biblical references, personal experiences, current events, theological concepts. But we will not preach *everything* that we uncover. A crucial rhetorical step is selecting what will be most appropriate for the situation and work the kind of persuasion we desire with the audience.

Rhetorical argumentation therefore, unlike formal logic, is directed toward the concrete and the practical with a particular people in mind. Nevertheless, it is still reasoned and analytical. Therefore, identifying issues and making choices are key rhetorical functions. The rhetorical approach provides us with a systematic way of working through all of these choices. Thus far we have discussed "How to come up with good reasons." Next we turn to the process of invention, the "how to come up with" portion of sermon invention.

INVENTION: GATHERING GOOD REASONS

When the ethnologist Bruce Rosenberg, who extensively studied the oral art of the American folk preacher, tried to ask his subjects about the sources of their ideas and the stories they used in their sermons, his otherwise talkative preachers just shook their heads. "I was told very early in my relationship with [the preachers] that there was no use talking about the preacher's language because it all came from God. That was the end of it. When I recorded a traditional folktale during one sermon the preacher was reluctant to discuss its source except in terms of the Holy Ghost."[8]

There may be moments like that of Isaiah when in our preaching, words come as if arising from lips purified by the hot coal. There may be moments like that of Moses, who was tending the flocks of his father-in-law and came on the extraordinary bush burning with the presence of God. And when we do discover God in unexpected places, like Moses did, we too become overwhelmed by God's love and awesomeness. Hopefully, our preaching grows out of such encounters with the divine. In conjunction with our own sense of call to proclaim the good news of God's gracious love, these encounters may encourage those first faltering efforts to speak on behalf of God. But unless we are like the preachers Rosenberg interviewed, most of us eventually have to admit that our ideas come from somewhere—we have to admit we are in this thing at least as deep as the Holy Spirit.

Rhetoric offers us ways of expanding our vision and opening our eyes to "all available means of persuasion." As we have observed in earlier chapters, your character and identity as a preacher are crucial to your task. You cannot, and should not, try to "get out of the way" of your message. There is no way that you can become a transparent or neutral vehicle for God's message. Nevertheless, we must, at the same time become aware of our limitations. In our discussion of *ethos* we pointed to the importance of the speaker, and this is no less true when it comes to *logos*. Your opinions and ideas are important when you are discovering and making choices. Since speakers are limited in their focus and even more limited in their comfort range of how to expand on ideas and stories, rhetoric's art of *logos* offers a means to broaden their vision and imagination.

The process of deciding on a theme, thesis, topic, or central idea, and developing supporting material for the claim in relation to a particular audience and specific situation is known as *inventio*, or *invention*. When classical rhetoricians spoke of invention they did not mean what we mean. We think of invention as making up something new—something that no one has thought of before. People invent devices that can be patented like lightbulbs, radio, television, or computers. But when you, as a speaker, begin the process of invention you are reviewing the options relative to possible topics or themes as they relate to the situation, the audience, and the goal to be achieved. Before you choose the evidence, stories, metaphors, images, or examples that will support or elucidate your claim, you want to make sure that you have considered all your options with reference to your basic concern.

Think of the process as akin to a preflight checklist. If you have ever been looking out a window at the airport you may have watched a pilot going through this process. Before a pilot takes off, whether it is in a small two-seater, or large airliner, there is a list of things to be checked both outside the plane and inside the cabin. By having a set order of reviewing everything, the pilot can be sure that he or she has examined every possibility.

So how do you begin? Where can invention take you? *Invention* offers three classic methods of getting started, three checklists for coming up with "good reasons" that force us to push beyond stereotyped thinking and what we think we know. Invention provides resources to analyze a situation or text, discover ways of thinking about it, and finally the impetus to select the most appropriate response.

Stasis

The first of our three methods of getting started is *stasis* theory. In antiquity, the *stasis* method was a system of questions developed among those in the legal profession that served as a checklist for determining the point of contention, the key question, about the most productive ways to develop a case. The word means "stopping point" and comes from the image of an arrow being stopped in mid-flight. By examining the trajectory at each point, the lawyer was able to make "course corrections" to keep the case on target. These were basic questions in the case or the point of disagreement. Did someone do something? If you were willing to admit that your client did perform the act, was it legal or not? What was the quality of the act? Was the killing in self-defense? And the question of last resort was, did this group of people have the right to pass judgment?

Obviously preachers do not need to ask a set of ancient forensic questions to get a sermon started. Nevertheless, a standard checklist of questions is a reasonable resource. These should be a set of questions you ask yourself to get things rolling. Some questions are obvious. Is this a special occasion, a particular season of the church year? Has anything tragic or wonderful happened in the congregation, the community, or the nation? Would preaching on this subject be especially sensitive for this congregation in any way? Less obvious questions are those which we bring to the task of translating exegesis into something that "preaches." We think preachers should work to make their implicit questions explicit and then examine them to see if they help make appropriate course corrections in the transition from exegesis to determining the issues or concern at stake in the sermon.

An example can help. When Bob approaches a text to be preached he asks the following five questions:

1. Did someone say something, do something, or does something happen in the text?
2. How is the identity or experience of God/gospel/grace/kingdom made evident in what is said, done, or happens a counterintuitive alternative to the consciousness of the dominant culture?
3. In what way is what is said, done, or happens similarly counterintuitive to the way contemporary culture sets up my *preunderstanding* about how just to get on and get by?
4. In communicating this insight how do I keep from pandering to the dominant cultural idolatries on one hand or religious dogmatism on the other?
5. Who am I called to be and what do I believe faith would look like as a result of navigating an appropriate response between these two extremes?

When preaching topically Bob adapts this process in the following manner:

1. Did someone say something, do something, did something happen, or is there a situation in the dominant culture of the world about which I believe God would have me speak?
2. Is the identity or experience of God/gospel/grace/kingdom revealed or obscured by what was said, what was done, in what happened, or in the situation?
3. How is a theological understanding of this topical event counterintuitive to a dominant cultural understanding—the kind of "understanding" that controls my *preunderstanding* about how to get on and get by?

4-5. These remain the same as those above.

Stasis questions such as these assist a preacher in negotiating what, in chapter 4, we called the rhetorical situation. In that chapter we spoke of the need to navigate between inadequate options in order to arrive at an appropriate response. Thus, to revisit the illustration we offered there, when addressing the death of a child in the congregation we allow the questions to save us from the empty word of cultural despair (for example, "All we can do is mourn this loss") or the simplistic response of religious dogmatism (for example, "God needed her more than we did"). Bob's questions allow him to suggest that an appropriate response would be to affirm that all of life is gift, pure and simple, something we neither earn nor deserve nor have a right to. So only when we approach life in this way can we accept that, even at the death of a beloved child, that the appropriate response to a gift, even one which is taken away, is still gratitude.[9]

The point is to develop your own set of *stasis* questions. Questions that you find challenging and that lead you to new and deeper insights. It should be a checklist that you can go through each time you begin to write a sermon. What is crucial for us to understand as we begin to think rhetorically is that, on most occasions, good speeches and good sermons do not appear by magic or sudden inspiration. They proceed out of your hard and careful investigation into discovering what is at stake in the heart of the matter and the materials/evidence that will move, support, challenge, comfort, enlighten, and enliven your listeners.

Topoi

Another method of approaching a new subject was to use topical reasoning. The *topoi* were lines of reasoning, or, put simply, another way of asking questions. According to Aristotle there are universal, or common, topics that help us to both formulate and to analyze most arguments. The common topics are definition, comparison, relationship, circumstance, and testimony. When an orator approached a new situation the *topoi* served as another systematic approach to investigating possible approaches.

• What is the definition of a word?

- What is the relationship between two groups?
- How do two situations compare?
- Is something possible, or impossible?

Think, for a moment, about the *topoi* of comparison, and how it can help us when we are thinking about a sermon on Acts 2 for Pentecost. Here is how it helps Lucy get started. Comparison asks about similarity and difference, about size, larger or smaller. After the coming of the Holy Spirit, the new church was *larger* and *stronger* than the small, frightened band of disciples that gathered in the upper room. When we recognize that we, as the church of God, have been brought into being by the same Spirit, we will realize that we are stronger than any of the powers of the world.

Modern rhetoricians often call *topoi* "suggesters" or "prompters." They provide ways of reasoning that reflect a rhetorical stance relevant to sorting out what is involved in an issue. Just like the pilot's checklist, they encourage us to move beyond idiosyncratic ways of thinking about a theme or text. The worst thing that a preacher can do is begin writing a sermon thinking that they "know the lesson already" or say "I've already got a sermon on that text." Remember, each time you approach a text, a theme, a topic, or a story, you are in a different moment than you were the last time you taught, preached, or thought about it. Your congregation is different, the situation is different, and so are you. Rhetorically it all calls for a fresh response.

Conversation Partners

The questions of *stasis* and the categories of the topics help us to identify, narrow, and sift through the wide range of options available to us. But we must also be aware that we are not the only ones involved in the conversation. In addition to questions and checklists, we need to open our hearts and minds to hear the voices of others, whether they are the voices of our listeners, our confessional tradition, theologians, the nonreligious, or, perhaps, marginalized voices that too easily fall below our horizon of awareness unless we seek them out. Listening to other voices becomes another way to discover what is at stake in the transition from exegesis to determining the direction a sermon will take in raising an issue or a concern. It turns "preaching as monologue" into "preaching as a conversation" where we collaborate with others as a community.

At the opening of this chapter we told of the experience of a pastor who realized that he needed to reframe a sermon when asked to preach for another community. He recognized the truth of *phronêsis*, the communal nature of rhetorical argumentation. The arguments and examples that would be persuasive in his home congregation might be heard differently in the other community. So he had to actively consider the concerns, questions, and opinions of this community as he rewrote the sermon.

Logos recognizes the communal nature of rhetoric, for our arguments are built on and must respond to the sense of the community. The topics and *stasis* questions are essentially internal brainstorming. Therefore, it is also crucial to draw on external sources in the preparation of sermons. We feel that it is important to note the importance of moving beyond the isolation of the study. This can happen in a number of ways. Many clergy are involved in sermon study groups with other clergy. Increasingly, clergy are forming sermon study groups with members of their congregation. But, preachers are able to get in touch with voices outside of their own community right in their own study. Expanding your reading beyond biblical commentaries to theological works and the spiritual writings by Christians from around the world will help you to realize the broader, global conversation that is going on around us.

In her preaching classes Lucy asks her students to list the conversation partners who inform, shape, and influence their sermons over the course of a week's preparation. On the average, most students bring in a list of four or five: some are members of the congregation, some are members of no congregations, some are family members, and, occasionally, some are even fellow clergy. The students become amazed as the blackboard fills with all the names of conversation partners. Few tend to be aware of just how great the "cloud of witnesses" are who tangibly contribute to sermons. But once these partners in theological conversation are listed, Lucy then solicits the names of other contributors that end up affecting the content of what gets said in the sermon: the news media, the entertainment industry, church officials, scholars, and politicians. The list grows and awareness of conversation partners grows with it.

Invention is all about opening your eyes and listening to where God is acting and moving in the world. It is about moving beyond the Acts 17:28 world of faith into the world in which most of us "live and move and have our being." Invention pushes us to seek the new and deeper insight, not settling for the first and easiest answer, realizing that rhetoric is a never ending process of searching and gathering. But it is also about finally taking a stand and making a choice. Invention is a process of fully examining the situation, collecting all relevant information, and finally making a selection about what you will and will not include based on your knowledge of yourself, of your congregation, and of God. The goal is to *tell* people in a way that they will be able to hear, not to *tell* people what they want to hear.

Stasis questions, topical reasoning, and conversational reflection are all ways to push into gear the process of "coming up with" what's at stake in the move between exegesis and sermon construction. They help the preacher come up with what counts as "good reasons." In the next chapter we will explore how strategies of arrangement can also function as part of this inventional process. In many ways, much recent homiletic theory has preferred to let the poetics of strategy perform part of the function of helping preachers figure out what they are going to say as a way of letting the form do the (indirect) work of persuasion rather than admitting that an argument is still being made. We have been blessed with a recovery of narrative ways of knowing. But argument is also an essential way of knowing. One need not turn to Aristotle to prove that. Just ask the rabbis.

FURTHERING THE CONVERSATION

As we have noted, argument has come in for hard times in recent preaching theory. It occurred as mainline homileticians began to realize that a heritage of continual schism and the start of so many new Protestant denominations in America may have been the product, in part, of rationalistic argument turned into a kind of debate theory *gone to seed*. Much of contemporary homiletic theory represents a justifiable reaction to the doctrinal *hairsplitting* of a previous generation's preaching style. It also represents, in ways we will take up in the next chapter, a very legitimate effort to respond to real changes in responding to what listeners view as relevant. Argument fell on hard times for good reason. Yet, we think one of the more unfortunate results of this reactionary posture is students can easily leave a modern course on preaching having arrived at the conclusion that offering anything that amounts to good reasons is nothing but manipulation. Many preachers, therefore, hide their "good reasons" in narratives, and their listeners are not aware that the preacher snuck a reason in on them. Still, other preachers present their reasons as options so that no one can accuse them of suggesting that some reasons are better than others.

A reinvigorated rhetorical stance in preaching helps us to see the importance of context and content when it comes to *logos*. Artistic use of *logos* demands that preachers consider a variety of possible choices, and then *make* a choice among them. That does not mean that we are forcing our listeners to mindlessly accept what we have to say. It means they will not be able to accept or reject our point of view unless we have been honest and clear with ourselves about what that point of view is. Therefore, preaching should not be afraid of *logos*. It does not obscure. Adopting a rhetorical stance toward *logos* is about making commitments to what we are trying to say.

As the people of *Logos*, the Word, we must be aware of the power of God's Word, the power of human words, and the power words have to create. We know the capability language has to build up and to destroy. Human words can bring comfort and healing, or they can injure and wound. The old childhood rhyme "Sticks and Stones..." is far from accurate. Words can be a vicious weapon. In fact, physical scars may heal much more quickly than the wounds inflicted by malicious and hateful language. This is why scripture is filled with stories and admonitions encouraging us to choose our words prayerfully and carefully, always aware of their tremendous power.

On the Question of Persuasion

In her book *Sharing the Word: Preaching in the Roundtable Church*, Lucy Rose has argued that preaching must not be viewed as persuasion because that would be inconsistent with a spirit of openness, mutual respect, and the search for inclusivity. She maintains that preaching should never adopt an authoritative, persuasive voice that assumes viewpoints that are "universal and normative." To adopt this kind of *voice* in preaching is not only individualistic and exclusive, but it is also hierarchical. It establishes a gap between the preacher and the congregation, and they become passive listeners who must accept this objective, propositional truth. "If the preacher's task is to teach, persuade, or change the congregation, the preacher and the congregation stand apart from each other."[10] Instead, she proposes that "preaching's goal within a community of equals is to facilitate the communal tasks of defining, maintaining, and reforming corporate identity and social order."[11] This rejection of persuasion is necessary because, "Persuasive preaching and leadership styles have been abusive to many in the church whose experiences and convictions have been consistently ignored or dismissed."[12]

• QUESTIONS FOR DISCUSSION

Lucy Rose is opposed to argument because it assumes an overpowering position of authority on behalf of the speaker. But can preachers engage listeners outside of the church if such a position is adopted? Or can people within the church be mobilized to take a stand against an injustice outside the church? David Buttrick rejects the argument that would make "identity-preservation" the goal of preaching. He finds that this kind of preaching says, "Let's tell our story. Let's preserve our tradition. Let's hunker down and hold onto ourselves in the name of the Lord." But the result is, "The gospel becomes the gospel of the church and 'the Word of the Lord is not heard in the land.'"[13] What do you think about the role of argument in preaching? Does it have a place? Take a position.

On Learning to Offer Good Reasons.

In our discussion of Toulmin we only presented what he calls the "first skeleton" for analyzing an argument.[14] Toulmin goes on to say that there are different kinds of warrants that have different degrees of force. For example, some warrants authorize unequivocal claims while some warrants only authorize tentative claims. And sometimes warrants require *backing* (B):

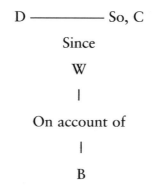

D ——————— So, C

Since

W

|

On account of

|

B

   In other words, good reasons, as we all know can become complex.[15] Most of us are accustomed to making claims through argument. When necessary we can supply the implicit warrants and backing for those warrants even though we may not have known the terminology to describe this kind of argument support. In this chapter we have suggested that discovering warrants in making and listening to arguments is crucial, because, according to Toulmin this is often the very point at which we disagree with a speaker or, as the speaker, we lose our listeners. This is because warrants are often implicit, which means that we depend on the listener to supply the warrant. We think preachers can be unaware of the warrants their sermons assume.

• QUESTIONS FOR DISCUSSION

Using a prearranged sermon or portion of a sermon try to find the key arguments and diagram them. Are the warrants explicit? Did they require backing? Are they implicit? Would all listeners agree?

READ MORE ABOUT IT

Kenneth Atchity. *A Writer's Time: A Guide to the Creative Process from Vision Through Revision.* New York: W. W. Norton, 1986.

Karlyn Kohrs Campbell. *The Rhetorical Act.* Belmont, Calif.: Wadsworth Publishing, 1996.

David S. Cunningham. *Faithful Persuasion.* Notre Dame: Notre Dame University Press, 1991.

John McClure. *Best Advice for Preaching.* Minneapolis: Fortress Press, 1998.

Gabrielle Lusser Rico. *Writing the Natural Way.* Los Angeles: J. P. Tarcher, 1983.

Chapter 6

What Do I Hope Will Happen?

Form is Formulation—the turning of content into a material entity, rendering a content accessible to others, giving it permanence, willing it to the race. Form is as varied as are the accidental meetings of nature. Form in art is as varied as idea itself.

—Ben Shahn, *The Shape of Content*[1]

I too decided, after investigating everything carefully from the very first, to write an orderly account for you, most excellent Theophilus, so that you may know the truth concerning the things about which you have been instructed.

—Luke 1:3-4

THE CHANGES IN THE PARADIGMS OF HOMILETIC ARRANGEMENT

TOM TROEGER SITS before his word processor to craft a brief wedding sermon for Catherine and Jonathan about what is involved in the vows of promise and covenant they are about to make. The result is a homily that anyone who has preached one of these sermons would recognize as a fine, even better than average, example of the genre. Yet Troeger is dissatisfied. This homily lacks something. Then he hits on it—it lacks the sense of immediacy that television has conditioned in viewers. The thing is idea heavy. So he begins to rethink the homily by asking, "How can I telecast what I have said rhetorically?" The result was a new homily that develops a series of images in which a couple, who reenact their wedding moment for a once-a-year photograph,

113

rediscover the meaning of the vows in the snapshots Troeger images across their years together. By the homily's end the story of the couple becomes a prayer of promise for Catherine and Jonathan as they make their vows.[2]

Troeger titles the former "A Sample Rhetorical Sermon for the Print Generation" and the latter "A Sample Visual Sermon for the Mass Media Generation." His frustration is just one example of the shift in homiletical thought that has occurred in preaching theory during the last quarter of the twentieth century. Many modern homileticians have reacted against the rationalism of Enlighten-ment rhetoric and, in an effort to supplant such logic-centered approaches, have attempted to discover ways of allow-ing image and narrative to play a larger role in creating experience as an event of meaning for listeners. This has been the epicenter of the paradigm shift in homiletic theory that has dom-inated the last quarter of the twentieth century. Troeger's example simply illustrates the kind of shift preachers are making as they learn to pay attention to what they desire to happen for listeners during the preaching event.

Recall from our discussion in chapter 2, the way contemporary homileticians are challenging preachers to realize what matters in preaching is not so much what the sermon is as what the sermon does. And what a sermon *does* is something that the preacher should be attuned to in designing the strategy that controls the sermon's compositional structure. In other words, choices in ser-mon pattern, whether intentional or intuitive, have direct conse-quences for a sermon's effect on listeners. Like the *means* of persuasion we have examined in the chapters before this, differ-ent strategies that can be used when arranging sermons are also part of the rhetorical resources available to the preacher. These approaches provide ways for a preacher to discover how to com-municate effectively within a range of desired responses. Most preachers learn one way to organize the strategy of a sermon, or tend to view the options as a choice between making a logical or a narrative presentation. In this chapter we want to assist preach-ers in adopting a rhetorical stance toward strategies of arrange-ment, which means we want to help them think about strategies of presentation as persuasive resources they have at their disposal that can help facilitate what they hope will happen as a response to the sermon.

From the beginning, the military metaphor *argument is war* has controlled the way we talk about arrangement. The Greek word for the idea, *taxis*, is even borrowed from the idea of marshaling troops on the battlefield. This is just one more example of the way that our language about these ideas shapes how we think about what is supposed to be happening as we preach. Some of the ways of controlling sermon design that we will talk about in this chapter are structured by language assumptions from the two millennia of thinking in terms of the *argument is war* metaphor (for example, strategy, etc.). Others are structured by newer ways of thinking of argument as a *process* (for example, as collaboration, as conversation, etc.). Since we are not advocating one approach over another in this book we make no attempt to choose one metaphor over another in this chapter either.

ARRANGEMENT THEORY AS RHETORICAL STRATEGY

The ancient dictum to "Deal with your subject; the words will fall into place" has been the mantra of plainspoken, content-oriented speakers since it was first uttered in the second century B.C. Aristotle's approach to the theory of arrangement is similar to this. The most noted historian of classical rhetoric, George Kennedy, admits that Aristotle's *Rhetoric* totally ignores the significance of arrangement theory in helping speakers to figure out what they want to say. After devoting two thirds of the *Rhetoric* to a discussion of the three means of persuasion, he treats the subject of arrangement in the final third "almost as an afterthought: as something expected in a discussion of rhetoric but of relatively little importance."[3]

On the other hand, Quintilian considered the role of arrangement in effecting persuasion to be far more important. He argued that, "The gift of arrangement is to oratory what generalship is to war. The skilled commander will know how to distribute his forces for battle, what troops to keep back to garrison forts or guard cities, to secure supplies, or guard communications, and what dispositions to make by land and by sea. But to possess this gift, our orator will require all the resources of nature, learning and industrious study."[4] Most ancient rhetoricians agreed with Quintilian rather than Aristotle. They considered trained judgment in knowing when and how to use the most effective argument something that could only be accomplished in concert with *a well-planned strategy of organization.* This was the essence of the orator's craft. Contemporary rhetorical theory acknowledges that the process of organization is an essential aspect of argument. The strategy by which speakers or writers structure ideas and make connections between them is considered an essential part of making an effective case or engaging listeners in an effective manner.[5] This is true whether the sermon is organized by a rational logic with the development of specific ideas controlled by a central thesis or by a narrative logic where ideas are expressed through the creation of an experience controlled by the design of a plot. When Bob teaches the public speaking course, he works to get students to become accustomed to thinking in terms of using preexisting patterns of arrangement (for example, topical, ethical, problem-solution, etc.) to structure the strategy of thought with a goal of realizing a specified purpose. More than just developing a thesis and arranging the content of what they want to say, Bob tries to get students to ask one of the following questions about the actual persuasive purpose:

- Do I want to convince listeners to accept a certain presentation or interpretation of the facts?

- Do I want listeners to affirm, reject, or appropriate the values of a certain worldview?

- Do I want listeners to act in order to implement a specific policy?

Rhetoricians call these "organizing questions" of fact, value, and policy.

Once a student decides which of these purposes she or he has in mind, it will have dramatic effect on how the speech will be organized. For example, a speech is organized by a question of fact when the speaker desires that listeners reach a verdict about something that has already occurred or a verdict about a particular construal of known information (for example, "The evidence the prosecution will present does not support the claim that my client is guilty," or "Balancing the federal budget is necessary for the following three reasons."). A speech is organized by a question of value when the speaker desires that the listeners make a choice between which worldview they approve among competing cultural options ("Granting marital rights to homosexual partners will challenge the very fabric of our cultural cohesiveness, but denying people their basic civil rights because it tears at the fabric is equally problematic."). A speech is organized by a question of policy when the speaker desires that the listeners adopt a specific course of action with regard to future behavior ("Sales of handguns to private citizens in the U.S. should be banned."). Of course, speeches will treat all three kinds of claims in the same speech. For example, a speech advocating the adoption of abortion legislation may be organized by a question of policy, but it cannot avoid dealing with questions of fact and questions of value.

Once the student has determined which of the three will serve as the primary organizing question of her or his speech, Bob tries to help them see how that choice already suggests which theory of arrangement will be most suitable in helping them achieve the desired purpose of the speech. Each organizing question has a preferred theory of arrangement already tailored to bring about the desired response, whether it be a verdict about the facts at issue, a choice among the competing values at issue, or action taken by listeners to enact or adopt a policy at issue. The fundamental question to be asked is: "How do I want listeners to respond?" "to render a verdict?" "to change their mind?" "or to take action?" Once this decision is made, the student need only realize that:

- a topical pattern best serves questions of fact helping listeners arrive at a verdict

- an ethical dilemma pattern (an exploration and balanced, thoughtful reflection that models a way of thinking through an issue) best serves a question of value helping listeners change their worldview.

- a problem-solution pattern best serves a question of policy moving listeners to take action.

We think preachers need to be asking a similar set of questions relevant to preaching: What do I want my listeners to do in response to this sermon? Once they have answered this question, they have a much clearer sense of the purpose of their sermon and what they hope will happen as listeners respond to having heard it. For this reason, preachers need a similar set of stock questions they can ask to help them choose the most effective strategy or means to collaborate in devising the arrangement of a sermon.

Preaching's Purposes and Its Range of Approaches

When it comes to the process of arranging the parts of a sermon, week after week most preachers use a combination of what they have learned by watching others, what they were taught to do in seminary, and an intuitive sense of what seemed to have worked well in their most recent sermons. In time, they develop stock ways into the subject of a sermon, for exploring the text, for deriving meaning, and for making their "so what" move. Occasionally, if they feel the need to try something a little different they may even turn to books that promise to offer an alternative, specialized approach to preaching. In addition, standard homiletic textbooks often include a brief section containing tried and true formulas from the "stockroom" or the "stockpile" of homiletic practice. Approaches are then named and briefly described. Very few of these books actually alert readers to the fact that stock approaches all come with a set of assumptions about the desired purpose of a sermon preached in this way.[6] The same thing is true concerning the stock approach each of us develops and the alternative approaches found in homiletic resources.

In other words, different ways of organizing the material achieve different purposes. Although this observation seems simple, it has some very significant implications.

For example, when it comes to asking questions about how to choose a way to structure the sermon we think preachers need to turn this process around. Instead of asking "what pattern should I use?" we think preachers should ask, "what response do I hope will occur as a result of listening to this sermon?" Patterns of organization are strategies or processes of elaboration that get us someplace. So, instead of choosing a mode of transportation and seeing where it will take us, we believe preachers should determine in advance where they hope to arrive and then pick the mode of transportation that is most apt to get them where they want to go. This is a different way of thinking, but preachers who learn to think in terms of letting the desired response shape the strategy of presentation are beginning to develop a rhetorical stance to arrangement theory in preaching.

We have already listed public speaking's purposes and the strategies that help listeners to get there. We believe preachers need to ask a different set of questions:

- Do I want to provide an *Explanation* of biblical truth?

- Do I want to facilitate an *Encounter* with God/Spirit/"the Lord"?

- Do I want to create an *Experience* making possible an event of meaning in which I do not control the final meaning to be derived?

- Do I want to explore ways to *Engage* the storied-identity of Christ or of God in a communal conversation that helps bring about Christian formation.

Each of these purposes have stock approaches closely identified with theories of preaching that help achieve the following set of *preaching intentions:*

- Affirming or reaffirming the validity of an *Explanation.*

- Specific, personal life choices are faced or made because of an *Encounter* with God/Spirit/the "Lord."

- New possibilities of understanding gospel and ways of being-in-world occur as a result of going through an *Experience* of meaning.

- Ways of experiencing solidarity with a faith community and solidarity with one's identity in Christ occur through *Engagement.*

Just as well-developed topical, problem-solution, and ethical speech patterns bring about distinctly different *desired responses* in traditional public speaking, we believe good sermons tailor choices at each moment in sermon construction to serve the chosen preaching intention. The preacher who is unclear about the function of any particular *point, development, move,* or *performance* is probably unclear or unfocused concerning the indivisible relationship between form and content. We are not suggesting that a sermon with a purpose to facilitate an encounter never offers any explanation, or never tries to create an experience of meaning, or never tries to perform an intention. As we indicated in our discussion of traditional public speaking theory above, questions of fact, questions of value, and questions of policy may arise as part of the development of any speech. They are not mutually exclusive concerns. The question is whether they advance the presentation's primary interest in achieving the specified *desired response.* And this is something we believe a preacher should be active in determining rather than allowing the form to accomplish this end by default.

Most contemporary preachers tend to use either the lectionary or to preach from a series of preselected biblical texts determined to be relevant to the congregational life. After the work of exegesis in which preachers seek to determine the action or the "to do" of what they believe a particular portion of scripture was trying to accomplish for its original listening audience, the real question becomes how to compose a sermon with a *preaching intention* aligned with the "to do" of the text for the listening audience. And it is here that the contemporary list of *preaching intentions* proves helpful. Once both exegetical intentions are determined with reference to the text, we believe the preacher needs to determine a *preaching intention* with regard to listeners: "Do I intend to provide an *explanation*, facilitate an *encounter*, create an *experience* of meaning, or explore the possibilities of *engagement* through the formative language of faith?" Only after this question is answered is it reasonable to assume that the preacher might look for an appropriate way of arranging the strategy of a sermon to help bring about the *desired responses*. These "patterns" and "strategies" range from the traditional three-points design motif that calls for a verdict to ways of plotting theological movements that call for a "going on" in faith.

SERMON PATTERNS THAT LEAD TO DESIRED RESPONSES

The four *preaching intentions* we have identified are derived from the four major approaches to preaching identified by homileticians at the close of the twentieth century. Each approach to preaching represents a very specific set of assumptions about the nature of truth and the purposes of preaching. They represent four different paradigms of preaching. Each approach tends to move toward an *intention* that supports its assumptions about the nature of truth and the way in which preaching can best assist listeners to respond in different ways to God's claim for them to be the people of God. The first two paradigms, the *Traditional* and the *Kerygmatic*, are well defined. The third paradigm represents a collection of approaches in which the creation of an experience of meaning appears to be the basis of productive unity. These approaches have been called the *New Homiletic* and the *Transformative* approaches, but we choose to refer to them as the *Practical Postmodern* approaches in order to differentiate them from the fourth, *Postliberal* paradigm, which we refer to as *Thoroughly Postmodern* preaching.

As with the relationship between patterns and different intentions in public speaking, each of these paradigms has its own patterns of preaching that have been developed to assist preachers in achieving that necessary *preaching intention*. In what follows, we try briefly to sketch the basic assumptions of each of these paradigms of preaching and the patterns of preaching that help preachers arrive at the appropriate *preaching intention* for each approach.[7]

The Traditional Approach to Preaching: Patterns of Explanation

A century after it was first written, Broadus's *On the Preparation and Delivery of Sermons* is still in print and use. It represents the seminal twentieth century text for the Traditional approach to preaching, the purpose of which is to persuade listeners "of the truth." In its present form, the Traditional approach views the function of preaching as inculcating and transmitting an explanation of Christian belief by eliciting assent to an explicit or implicit doctrinal formulation, by challenging an alternative doctrine, worldview, or ideology, or simply by persuading listeners to act kindly, justly, or Christianly. This approach tends to be framed by either a creedal orthodoxy or a propositional formulation of faith as biblical "Truth." The authority of the preacher in this approach resides with his or her credibility in serving the role of official arbiter of "revealed truth." In the Traditional approach the preacher tries to provide answers that, if accepted, secure the listener's identity as adherents to the creedal tradition or to the particular theology. With its strong ties to the rationalist rhetorical tradition, this kind of preaching borrows the most from the thematic presentations which the speaker argues "points." This is preaching as Explanation in which the purpose is to have listeners render a verdict by affirming or reaffirming their belief in the conclusions or propositions presented.

Of the four approaches, this kind of sermon borrows the most from traditional public speaking forms. Whether the purpose is to explain an idea, prove a proposition, apply a principle, develop a theme, use story to make a point, or motivate a congregation to act on a belief, many of the approaches are simply adaptations of existing *topical, problem-solution,* or *ethical* speech patterns adapted to the interpretation of a text.

The Topical Pattern. The *Topical* arrangement is not to be confused with a topical sermon. The former is a way of logically structuring the argument of a sermon with "points" to be made, while the latter is a kind of sermon that offers an interpretation of a cultural concern from a biblical perspective. Topically arranged preaching is the classic expression of the didactic sermon in which a thesis (e.g., the Centrality of Faith) is then developed by a series of main points (Its power... Its purpose... Its promise).

Expository Pattern. Verse by verse expository preaching is just a variation of this. The goal is still an explanation of however many textual points the preacher chooses to address. This sermon style usually extracts implications as "points" from the biblical material. Other variations on this pattern include the *Chronological* and the *Causal* patterns. For example, an expository *Chronological* approach generally provides running commentary explaining the "then" and "now" meaning of a preselected set of sequential verses. Other uses of the *Chronological* tend to pursue an idea as an aspect of time or sequence (e.g., the historical development of a biblical theme or the steps necessary to achieve a spiritual goal). *Causal* sermons tend to develop a claim with an "If... then..." formula. Often this form creates suspense by withholding the full development of the claim or thesis until the "if" has been fully explored. The *desired response* of all these variations on the *Topical Pattern* is to have listeners render a verdict by affirming or reaffirming their belief in the explanations presented.

The Problem-Solution Pattern. This is often presented theologically as a "law-gospel" sermon. Some facet or aspect of the "law" of God is presented as the problem or dilemma humans face with the goal of acting to accept the gospel as the solution to a sinful condition. The *desired response* is for listeners to act by accepting the redemptive promise of the gospel.

The Ethical Pattern. This form is often described as the "indicative-imperative" pattern. This style of sermon is structured first by an exposition of the claims of the text and then an exploration of the "ought" the preacher derives as its contemporary application. An alternative is to present an accepted cultural perspective and then counter its claim by presenting the counterclaim of the gospel as a new way to live. The *desired response* is for listeners to rethink and reorient ways of interpreting the relationship between faith and cultural commitments.

The Kerygmatic Approach to Preaching: Patterns of Encounter

Kerygmatic preaching was significantly influenced by C. H. Dodd's effort to identify the essential content of the gospel preached in the New Testament, by the nonpropositional theology of German *heilsgeschichtlich* theology. This approach to interpretation views revelation, not as a body of truths about God, but the very presence of God revealed in salvation history, and by the introduction of the more subjective "therapeutic model" of preaching which redefined faith psychologically as "meeting people's needs." In its contemporary form the Kerygmatic approach views the function of preaching as providing an opportunity for the listener to have an encounter with God and the demands of the gospel. In this approach, greater attention is given to the exposition and application of a theme derived from a specific text in the belief that it can provide the opportunity for the individual to have an encounter with God's active, redemptive presence. The authority of the preacher in this approach resides with his or her credibility in providing an interpretive, existentially relevant application of a particular text. In the Kerygmatic approach the preacher emphasizes the individual's ability to have an encounter with God in the context of a community of faith. The primary difference between Traditional preaching and

Kerygmatic preaching is that the latter is concerned to identify truth through the experience of facilitating an encounter with God and God's Word.[8]

Sermons in this approach are viewed as being biblical and their rationality becomes a seamless support rather than the visible structure of points or ideas. In this approach, preaching is understood as a communicative event in which listeners personally encounter the redemptive activity of God whether the sermon form begins with the felt need in human experience and moves to God's response in the sermon text, or it begins with God's redemptive activity in the sermon text and then applies it to a contemporary situation.

Kerygmatic Preaching that begins with the Listener's Experience. The contemporary form of Kerygmatic life-situation preaching mixed with careful exposition begins by empathetically creating identification with the individual's personal situation or need and demonstrates how God's saving activity can address that concern. The contemporary preacher, Lloyd Ogilvie, proposes the following pattern to organize the development of this kind of sermon: (1) Identification, (2) Interpretation, (3) Implication, (4) Implementation, and (5) Inspiration.[9] There is a significant parallel between this kind of patterned arrangement and the Motivated Sequence arrangement in public speaking theory. The latter is a highly focused speech pattern developed in five discrete steps and based on the psychology of individual persuasion: (1) gain focused attention; (2) establish the individual's need; (3) present the plan that satisfies the need; (4) visualize the benefits of adopting the plan; (5) inspire listeners to act.[10] The flow of both Ogilvie's and the Motivated Sequence's arrangement motivates listeners to act on the benefits proposed. In many ways, Ogilvie's sermon pattern is similar to a Traditional Expository pattern in that it still draws implied points from an exposition. The primary difference between this pattern and a Traditional *expository* pattern is that this kind of approach emphasizes the creation of a personal *Encounter* through "Identification" rather than clarifying "Implications" of a doctrinal truth.

Kerygmatic Preaching that begins with a Narrative Retelling of the Text. Whether the material preached is a narrative, moral exhortation, or prophetic pronouncement, the goal of this kind of preaching begins with the text and then moves toward applying an interpretation to a present context. It is rooted in creating a contemporary identification between the situation that called forth the text's initial redemptive response and the contemporary situation. For example, Henry Mitchell notes that a hallmark of black preaching style is a narrative form of retelling the whole of a Bible story in contemporary vernacular, often characterized by imaginative elaboration.[11] Paul Wilson has recently proposed a pattern of arrangement he calls the "four pages of preaching" approach. It represents an effort to facilitate the listener's identification with God's action in the text by making the connection between the concerns of the text and the concerns of the listener's life. The structure of the sermon is controlled by the following, roughly equal moves: (1) What is the trouble in the text? (2) What is similarly wrong today? (3) What is God's gracious action in or behind the text? (4) What is God's similar gracious action today?[12]

The primary difference between this approach and the Traditional approach's version of the Problem-Solution pattern is that the Kerygmatic approaches are more concerned with making the Bible story our story so that we will respond appropriately as the people of God. The *desired response* of this kind of preaching is to make the Bible story *my* story by facilitating the possibility of an *encounter* with the redemptive message of the Kerygma. Kerygmatic approaches that begin with the sermon text rather than the human situation can have significant overlap with Practical Postmodern approaches, but they differ in the degree to which they are willing to tell what the "redemptive" point is that is derived from the retelling of the biblical story.

The Practical Postmodern Approach to Preaching: Patterns of Creating Experience

Craddock's *As One Without Authority: Essays on Inductive Preaching* is often identified as the book that galvanized the shift away from the rationalist presuppositions that control both the Traditional and Kerygmatic approaches to preaching. Other homileticians of what became known as the New Homiletics developed narrative or storytelling forms of preaching and still other methods shaped by the movement and structure of thought in the biblical text to be preached. These diverse strategies represent an awareness of the significance of form as a means of affecting listeners.[13] These approaches all share a basic social constructivist perspective that meaning is collaboratively arrived at as part of the "language event" of preaching in which language is understood to function as an interpretive grid through which the constructed world and its worldview are shaped.

This approach views the function of preaching as an opportunity for the listener to experience an event of meaning in which the individual discovers a way of being-in-the-world transformed by gospel. To varying degrees, this approach is shaped by the European tradition of philosophical hermeneutics, in which the role of interpretive language is understood as a way of unfolding the possible meanings of being-in-the-world leading to understanding that one philosopher has described as an experience of second naïveté.[14] The authority of the preacher in this approach resides with his or her credibility in communicating a "wrestling with the text" as a way of discovering the gospel's transforming possibilities of being-in-the-world. In the Practical Postmodern approach, the preacher uses language to provide the means for an individual to have an experience of meaning that centers or recenters the life of faith. Practical Postmodern preachers are aware that the question of "meaning" is hermeneutically complex. They acknowledge that texts exert control over the limits of reasonable interpretations, but they are equally aware that "meaning" is limited by what the reader or listener brings to the process of interpretation. Practical Postmodern approaches have attempted to internalize the kind of hermeneutic in which, "The merely historicizing question—what did the text say?—remains under the control of the properly hermeneutical question— what does the text say to me and what do I say to the text?"[15] Patterns in this approach tend to reflect the preacher's own wrestling with this question of interpretation and how to assist listeners in experiencing a communal consciousness in meaning making. For example:

Indirection through Narrative Forms. McClure suggests that Craddock's and Lowry's organizational strategies for letting listeners interactively join in on the experience of wrestling and discovering meaning is a proposal of sermon forms that model an interdependency in the act of "problem solving." He describes the movement of both patterns as functionally similar: "Sermons [in these modes] are energized by a problem, a dis-equilibrium, a search, or an enigma. Something is wrong and needs fixing, something is out of balance and needs restoration, something is missing and needs to be found, something is confusing and needs to be clarified."[16] Lowry's "stages of the homiletical plot" are (1) Upsetting the Equilibrium, (2) Analyzing the Discrepancy, (3) Disclosing the Clue to Resolution, (4) Experiencing the Gospel, and (5) Anticipating the Consequences.[17] *The desired response* of these patterns of sermon development is that listeners participate in the puzzle of meaning and arrive at a personally relevant insight of gospel understanding.

Buttrick's Moves and the Three Modes. Buttrick offers an alternative to the "puzzle" approach that is also sensitive to the issues of how meaning gets determined. Rather than "arguing points," he calls for imaging a sermon through a series of moves that places the preacher's focus on whether the design helps the audience "get the idea." Moves are rhetorically designed stratagems by which the preacher shapes an idea so that it can form in the consciousness of an audience much as a gestalt is imaged in the process of human understanding. An individual move within a sermon (a typical sermon has five to seven moves) must be characterized by only one such rhetorical operation because the purpose of the move is the formation of a single understanding. He maintains that actual structure is derived from the rhetorical purpose of the sermon and the relationship between "text" and the proposed contemporary field of understanding. He does not limit the word "text" to biblical texts, because he contends that preaching is both a hermeneutic of biblical texts and a hermeneutic of human situations. So in organizing the structure of a sermon, the speaker must first develop a "field of understanding of a text," which is to say a convictional understanding of a *text's* contemporary meaning. Then this contemporary field of meaning is structured in one of three ways of preaching: in the *mode of praxis*, in the *reflective mode*, and in the *mode of immediacy*. The *desired response* of preaching in these modes is to assist the audience in the movement of their own convictional understanding such that they do not "feel they are being talked to so much as having a conceptual meaning form in consciousness as their own thought process."[18]

Whether the process is one of indirection,[19] plotting, or imaging an idea, the preacher still attempts to control the range of possible interpretations that can be appropriately derived from the sermon—which means that there is still an "Aha!" that can be propositionally formulated hiding coyly in the folds of the sermonic skirt. Yet this kind of preaching respects the listeners by inviting them on a journey of discovery in which they determine whether the experience of meaning is one with which they can identify.

The Thoroughly Postmodern Approach to Preaching: The Patterns of Formative Engagement

In what they would see as the aftermath of modernity's demise, postliberal preaching has emerged as a Thoroughly Postmodern approach. It has historic ties to both Karl Barth and Augustine, especially in the way postliberals reject the role of trying to prove the sensibility of Christian faith or justify its believability as a rational choice. The approach is decidedly postmodern, because its proponents view foundationalist rationality as "in ruins." Though postliberals may have differences of opinion about how to assess truth claims in the Bible, there would be common affirmation of the proposition that scripture offers the narrative of

God's storied identity and that preaching's purpose is to assist congregations in forming their own identity out of that revelation. Lindbeck, Frei, and Placher are among the important theologians whose inquiry structures this approach, with Hauerwas and Willimon, Lischer, Ellingsen, and Campbell as significant exponents of its shape as homiletic practice.[20] In many ways, postliberal preaching is a very intentional effort to recover a premodern Augustinian intelligibility (Placher), but make no mistake, this neo-fideism is thoroughly postmodern. The postliberal or Thoroughly Postmodern approach views the function of preaching as an engagement of the faithful in an expression of the solidarity already present between preacher and worshipers as they seek to accomplish the tasks of defining, maintaining, and reforming corporate identity and ordering social life in the storied identity of God revealed in scripture. This approach tends to view the task of preaching as creating communal identity through "Christian formation" and "performance" rather than as an "event of meaning" or "act of translation."[21] The preacher explores Christian claims as they are expressed in scripture and tradition and engages the community in a conversation about the implications for faith. The authority of the preacher in this approach occurs through performance. Rather than viewing preaching as one person attempting to persuade listeners, this approach offers the preacher as model, performing the Christian story before a community who then enact that story as their own performance.[22] In the Thoroughly Postmodern approach, preaching is a function of Christian formation in which the preacher uses language to engage the faithful community with an understanding of the implications of their redemption in Jesus Christ. Postliberal preaching is concerned with helping to form Christian identity and teaching the community to use its own language appropriately in contemporary contexts.

As Christian Formation. Distinctly Postliberal approaches to preaching tend to begin with the biblical text and then move to interpreting possible implications in the contemporary situation with the goal that preaching be viewed as performance of the church's peculiar language rather than translation of it. Sermon form can vary but usually moves toward providing listeners with ways of appropriating the language of faith that assist them in "going on" with it. Lischer maintains that the basic form of a sermon is a dialectical encounter between law and grace/gospel that begins with the biblical text and then moves to apply its peculiar language to the church's contemporary context: the movement tends to go through Analysis, Transition, and finally, Integration.[23] But the goal is not to have one person trying to persuade other persons, but, rather, to allow preaching for the church to speak *to* the church. The *desired response* is for preaching to use the language of faith to form a faithful community in which listeners hear and begin "to experience the possibility of integration that belongs to those who have exchanged death for life."[24]

Campbell calls for preaching that begins with the biblical narrative and moves to the contemporary situation and that, in the process, the sermon should enact on behalf of the community the particularity of Jesus as a performance of his storied identity. This kind of preaching enacts his storied kind of "counter-imagery, a counter-speech, which both resists and challenges cultural imagery of domination and subordination."[25] It models the process of "going on" as an improvisation on the language of Scripture and tradition played out in our own stories, but a kind of developmental improvisation that can only come about when we have learned how to use our language rightly.[26]

Because most of the theorists of this approach view "patterns" as structures that enact explicit or implicit persuasive hierarchies they are reluctant to identify specific forms or strategies other than those which enact the language of Scripture and tradition in the biblical story as a way of discovering how to be the community of faith now. The desired response is that the community engages the language of faith in such a way that they can act as people of faith in their own cultural moment.

Form and the Form of Faith

We want to underscore once again the indivisible relationship between form and content. By this we mean that form shapes the persuasive strategy every bit as much as the content of what is said. Craddock reminds us that well-structured form, gains and holds interest, determines the degree of participation demanded of hearers, shapes the listener's experience of the material, and shapes the listener's faith. Form is never neutral. It is an active agent rather than a passive container in preaching.

Craddock also proposes that, "As a frame does for a picture, the pattern for the sermon serves to arrest, accent, focus, and aid the listener's apprehension of the message."[27] We agree that the form, even existing patterns, serves the latter function, but we suggest that more than being a container, form is the very theory of *compositional representation*. As we discussed this, Lucy suggested that we take on the metaphor itself. She urged that we needed to say the function of arrangement *is* the same as the approach to artistic representation that gets expressed in a painting. It may be controlled by an early-, high-, or late-baroque approach, or a colorful burst of short brushstrokes of the late-nineteenth-century impressionist approach, or a complete lack of representation in mid-twentieth-century abstract expressionism. So rather than serving as a "frame," we say that it is this interaction of the compositional approach and the way it represents content that "serves to arrest, accent, focus, and aid the listener's apprehension of the message" being represented. The form in which the expressed content of a sermon is represented *is* the active ingredient fundamental to both its experience and the way in which it *enacts* the faith of its listeners.

This is why we suggest that the preacher who understands the language assumptions that structure the different approaches is more likely to be able to understand how strategies of arrangement serve to bring about *desired responses*. We hasten to recognize, however, that few preachers would likely be equally comfortable with the assumptions that underlie all of these approaches. This is why simply making lists of "stock" approaches is inadequate. But we also suspect that most preachers do adapt to different audiences and different preaching contexts such that they can make occasional use of the approaches to the immediate right or immediate left of their preferred approach. What would be inappropriate is to treat form as if it is little more than recipe. We would not do this when talking about approaches to representation in painting, nor should we do it in talking about approaches to preaching.

FURTHERING THE CONVERSATION

Understood aright, recipes have a place in helping people learn how to find their own voice in shaping a strategy for what they hope will happen in a sermon. One of the modern heirs of the ancient rhetorical handbook tradition might just be the cookbook. Recipes abound in both. As a mature rhetorician, Cicero was embarrassed at having written one of these cookbooks when he was young. He concluded that the problem with cookbook approaches applied to human situations is that they lack the subtlety necessary for speakers to be adept at making use of technical artistry in actual speaking situations. Of course the supple, sophisticated conception of rhetorical adaptation Cicero reveals in his mature essays requires the assimilation and mastery of the kind of principles he presented as a taxonomy in his youthful work. Good cooks first learn and follow the principles of cooking before they find the freedom to become chefs.

Our purpose in this chapter has been to refocus the "recipe" approach toward theories of arrangement. Understanding how form functions in relationship to achieving a *desired response* shifts the dynamic away from "recipes revealed" to providing preachers with principles for marrying form and content to achieve a *desired response* in specific rhetorical situations. Good sermon form is a unity between scripture and theology applied to particular rhetorical situations to achieve *desired responses*.

We have raised a number of issues in this chapter about viewing strategies of arrangement as part of the rhetorical resources available to the preacher. As you work to develop a rhetorical stance in preaching, it helps if you are able to engage in considered reflection and discussion of some of these ideas The following sections contain three questions we find worthy of this continued attention.

Arrangement Theory and Language Assumptions

Though it may surprise many preachers, their preferences in the strategy of sermonic composition rhetorically reveal their working assumptions about the nature of truth and how they believe the authority of a preacher should be conveyed. Ways of presenting "truth" in preaching range across a spectrum from the Traditional approach's assumptions of "objective truth" to Postliberal approach's assumptions of "discursive truth." Similarly, ways of expressing authority range from the Traditional preacher making claims *ex cathedra* about biblical texts to the Postliberal preacher plotting ways for listeners to "go on" in faith. Where a Traditionalist preacher holds that "a specifically homiletic use of scripture . . . would distill out of God's revelation in other times the timeless truth for all times,"[28] a Postliberal preacher contends that preachers and congregations increasingly will not be searching for truth "behind the text" because "the modern notion of truth as delimited to historical reference is of diminishing 'purchase' in a postliberal age."[29]

• QUESTIONS FOR GROUP DISCUSSION

Given the two ends of the spectrum presented here, discuss what the perspectives on "truth" and "authority" would be for the Kerygmatic and Practical Postmodern approaches. Then, find yourself (your approach to preaching) in the spectrum and see if it coheres with your own conception of the nature of truth, authority, and the response you hope will happen as a result of your having preached.

Finding the Balance

We noted in chapter 1 that many contemporary homileticians have tended to vilify rhetoric even to the point of wondering aloud whether there is a continued place for it. Most of these homileticians believe that in moving the emphasis in preaching away from *logos* to *arrangement* and *form*, they have chosen poetics over rhetoric. Both Lucy and Bob see it more as an in-house move, relocating preaching's purposes out of an Enlightenment view of *logos* as "means of persuasion" in favor of emphasizing the power of *arrangement* to function as a "means of persuasion." So we think the debate is somewhat disingenuous.

• QUESTIONS FOR GROUP DISCUSSION

Read the two essays of Craddock and Long in the "Read More About It" section of chapter 1 and take a position. What are the arguments that homiletic benefits from being severed from rhetoric? What gets lost if preaching is not a "kindred" art of rhetoric?

On the Form of Preaching and the Form of Faith

Craddock claims that form is never neutral and that, as a steady diet, it even shapes how listeners learn to respond with faith. We have named a set of *preaching intentions* (Explanation, Encounter, Experience, and Engagement) served by various forms in this chapter. Building on Craddock's claim, this suggests that people who listen to a steady diet of one way of shaping sermons will be strongly influenced to come to terms with faith in one or the other of the ways it has been regularly represented to them. We think the questions that arise from our analogy comparing representational form in preaching and representational form in painting worth further reflection.

• QUESTIONS FOR GROUP DISCUSSION

Is there a need to vary the form of representation, to have variety in desired responses? Is it even possible? Or do preachers, like painters, practice to become a master of one approach? What implications would consistently practicing only one approach have on the way faith gets "enacted" by listeners? What implications would practicing a great variety of approaches have on the way faith gets "enacted" by listeners?

READ MORE ABOUT IT

Richard Eslinger. *A New Hearing: Living Options in Homiletic Method.* Nashville: Abingdon Press, 1987.

Donald K. McKim. *The Bible in Theology and Preaching.* Nashville: Abingdon Press, 1994.

Lucy Atkinson Rose. *Sharing the Word: Preaching in the Roundtable Church.* Louisville: Westminster John Knox Press, 1997.

Paul S. Wilson. *Imagination of the Heart: New Understandings in Preaching.* Nashville: Abingdon Press, 1988.

Chapter 7

How Will It Come Across?

Thought and speech are inseparable from each other. Matter and expression are parts of one: *style is a thinking out into language.*
> —John Henry Newman, *The Idea of a University*[1]

The wise of heart is called perceptive, and pleasant speech increases persuasiveness.
> —Proverbs 16:21

AFTER PULPIT GIANTS?

IF YOU HAVE HAD occasion to visit Trinity Church in Boston, you may have had the humbling reaction that Lucy had as she walked into the vast and imposing sanctuary. Walking down the center aisle of Trinity she realized that it was unlikely any congregation would ever "build" a church in order to hear her preach.

In the nineteenth century there were giants in the land: Charles Spurgeon in England, and Henry Ward Beecher, Phillips Brooks, Alexander MacLaren, C. A. Tindley, and C. T. Walker in the U.S. By the middle of the twentieth century Harry Emerson Fosdick had only just retired as the century's preeminent "pulpiteer." These men were famous not only within, but without the church as well. Even if you did not attend Trinity in Boston or Riverside in New York, the powerful messages of Brooks or Fosdick were etched into the public consciousness. In fact, when Phillips Brooks died in 1893, tens of thousands of people formed his funeral procession.

Donald Macleod has noted that with few exceptions the time of the great "pulpiteer" has passed.[2] Occasionally someone could still point to, say, a Carlyle Marney or Gardner Taylor holding forth in the third quarter of the twentieth century, but the concept of "pulpiteer" has given way to something else. Great preaching still occurs, but the word "pulpiteer" evokes the image of a certain kind of eloquence most contemporary preachers find alien. In part all of this is a phenomenon of the restructuring of American religion that has been occurring since World War II. Sociologists of religion point to the growth of the small group movement as just one of many evidences of the decentralization of the "pulpit." Americans have widened their net in search of the sacred.[3]

It is also an effect of the general loss of constituency for the kind of spaciousness of the *grand* style of rhetorical speech that was the hallmark of eighteenth- and nineteenth-century oratory. Our forebears in previous centuries would travel for hours just to have a chance to hear the likes of John Hancock, Edmund Randolph, Henry Clay, John C. Calhoun, Daniel Webster, and Edward Everett. They were Ciceronian-like orators whose styles created commanding personas that were larger than life. They carefully chose their words, their figures of speech, the rhythm of their address to create a symphonic experience. Sweeping back and forth from a *plain* style to a *grand*, then to a *temperate* style, concluding with nothing less than a masterful *peroration*. Whether they were pulpiteers or orators, the ability to modulate between the *plain, temperate*, and *grand* styles of speech were the hallmarks of a kind of spacious rhetoric revered in a bygone era. It was a time when speakers assumed that their audiences shared a common morality, a common heritage, and belief in the common good.[4] With every passing decade in the twentieth century we discovered that this assumption proved increasingly less accurate.

In taking up the subject of style we ask ourselves the question, How will it come across? We express no yearning for the glory days of the pulpiteer. Gone is the culture in which listeners share a common identity. There is no single kind of pulpit voice that will reestablish that mythic American ideal or even that mythic

Christian ideal. Both in the political arena and in the church, spacious rhetoric that features a grand style is rarely heard. It would, however, be a mistake to equate attention to questions about style with these outmoded rhetorical forms.

Unfortunately, much of recent preaching theory still treats style as something very personal, as a means of ornamentation, or simply an issue of delivery. Stylistic concerns are not inconsequential or extraneous fluff. In this chapter we present a case for the idea that style is more than just finding one's idiosyncratic stamp or "dressing up" a sermon. We depart from an Aristotelian approach to our subject to argue that style, like arrangement theory, can help preachers generate what they want to say. We believe style involves a way of thinking as well as a way of connecting with a congregation. As Cardinal Newman so eloquently phrased it, "style is thinking out into language."

Fundamentals of Style: The "Signature" of Speech

You have completed your exegesis of the text and the context. You have come up with your central idea, your theme, your topic. You have developed your arguments and thought of several examples and illustrations. You have decided upon the arrangement of your sermon. Yet the questions still linger, "How will I draw people in when I begin? How will I order my arguments, my images, and illustrations? What kind of conclusion will send them out to do God's will?" And aside from these questions you are still wondering, "Should the style of the sermon be formal, casual, personal, or prophetic? Should the language reach for the evocative? Should it polish words to command stimulated engagement? Should it express uncommon possibilities in common speech?" And what of figures of speech and cadence? "Should metaphors control any part of the speech? Should imagistic language frame ideas? Should rhythm play a role?" Stylistic decisions, one and all.

What we say cannot be separated from how we say it. Just as classical composers or rock bands each have a distinctive style, or painters have an immediately recognizable *élan*, each of us has a distinctive "signature" of speech. We have certain words that we use, as well as others that we never use. We have rhythms, patterns, cadences, that all make our speech distinctive and recognizable. Some are peculiar to us as an individual, others to a particular region or language group. Bob's father was in the military and he lived alternately in both Northeast and Southwest coastal states for much of his childhood. As a result he tends to speak very standard English. Lucy, on the other hand, is originally from Minnesota. When she moved to Virginia twenty years ago people knew that she was *not* from "ole Virginny" by phrases she used, the lilt of her speech, and the pitch of her voice.

While we may have unconscious "stylistic fingerprints," we also make conscious stylistic decisions all day, every day. From the moment we get up in the morning until we go to bed at night we are adjusting what we say to the person or persons to whom we speak. If you are the parent of small children, or you work with young children, you know that you do not speak to them the way that you speak to a church council or the clerk in a store. While we certainly are not advocating that you speak "babytalk" when you are speaking to children, you must simplify your vocabulary, use more repetition, and employ a variety of illustrations. All of these strategies are designed to make sure that the child or children understand you. And, as strategies with a goal of bringing about understanding, they are efforts at persuasion.

How do we persuade another? Do we persuade by substance, the content of the arguments that we make? In other words, by the *meaning* of the words? Or do we persuade by style, the sound of the words and figures of speech? While for some this is an "either/or" question, we would argue that it is a "both/and." From the earliest rhetorical theories onward, the debate over the focus on content or style has taken a prominent place. While some theorists such as Aristotle tried to keep issues of style confined to what we would call a basic "no-frills" language usage, nevertheless, speakers still discovered early on that elegantly expressed speeches proved very persuasive.

Two important ways that ancient rhetoricians distinguished persuasive elements of style was by recognizing that different kinds of speaking situations called for different expressions of forcefulness and by comprehending that excellence could be achieved in each of them. These two different ways of thinking about style were reduced to what the ancients called "systems" or theoretical treatments of teachable art. One system was known as the levels or "Three Types of Style." The other system was known as the "Five Sources of the Sublime."

The Three Types of Style

Think of the character of the sermon that you would prepare for the principal Easter service. The church will be full to overflowing with people who are a crucial part of the congregation year in and year out, as well as visitors and returning family members who rarely, if ever, go to church. Now, compare that to the type of message you would prepare for the outdoor service that will kick off "Church Picnic Sunday." Everyone, children and adults alike, will be in their casual clothes, the food on the picnic tables will be beckoning, and the younger members of the congregation will have a difficult time sitting still.

You compose these two sermons differently because the contexts and the congregations are different. The first will probably be longer, comparatively more formal, while the second will likely be more casual. We hope you don't bring a manuscript to the picnic. We suspect many will even choose to forgo an outline. It will definitely be shorter. Let's face it, no one wants dry, cold, or overcooked hamburgers. Depending on your purpose the former may be a version of the grand or the tempered, middle style. The latter is undoubtedly a version of the plain style.

By the first century B.C. these three levels of style had been described and defined. Cicero offers the most efficient explanation: "He, then, will be an eloquent speaker...who can discuss [factual] matters in a *plain* style, matters of moderate significance in the *tempered* style, and weighty affairs in the *grand* manner."[5] Good speakers, he argued, were able to modulate between these "types" or levels of speaking by emphasizing different resources within the Virtues of Style system. These resources included use of correct grammar, clarity of expression, appropriate word arrangement, and skill in the use of figurative embellishments. Depending on the circumstance that called forth a speech, a speaker might want to maintain one type of style throughout a speech, while other speeches might call for skill in shifting among these types as the need and the moment required.

Just how eloquent a speaker should try to be was the basis of a volatile theoretical debate in the first centuries B.C. and A.D.[6] After Cicero, Augustan orators tended to prefer a kind of stoic just-the-facts minimalism in civic address. The *plain* style became the preferred Augustan style, while many speakers from Greece and Asia preferred the kind of oratory that Cicero had honed to an art. The latter were more appreciative of showmanship, often preferring it to speeches based on nothing more than clear arguments. For example, the apostle Paul was a master of the reasoned response, but notice how the Corinthian Christians were apparently comparing his speaking style to that of the people he called the "super-apostles" (2 Cor. 11:5). In response, Paul felt compelled to complain that, "I may be untrained in speech, but not in knowledge" (2 Cor. 11:6). This suggests that these "super-apostles" were probably masters of what some Greek rhetoricians called Asianist oratory. Speakers who used this style of presentation preferred to persuade listeners in *grand* style rather than persuading them through the use of well-reasoned arguments.

A recent book, *Best Advice for Preaching*, includes the observation by Barbara Brown Taylor that people in the pew value, "Genuineness in presentation, clarity of thought, appropriate humor, faithfulness to the biblical text, attention to the sacred dimensions of everyday life and imaginative language."[7] Sounds like good advice. It also sounds like updated advice of the Aristotelian Virtues of Style system. Aristotle advocated that a speech should demonstrate the following stylistic virtues: clarity, appropriateness, grammatical correctness, and ornamentation.[8] In other words, audiences have not changed that much. There is still as much appreciation out there for a "showman" as there is for a good argument. In fact, just as Paul discovered, even good Christians can be seduced into preferring the former. Is the alternative to let the plain style be the only standard?

The Five Sources of the Sublime

In the battle between substance and style, one anonymous Greek writer in the first century A.D. wrote a treatise on the necessity of mastering both. He titled the work *On the Sublime*. It was his opinion that control of style as a means of persuasion is necessary not only to help any writer develop power and intensity of thought, but also to express it sublimely. Here is how he describes the "Five Sources of the Sublime" necessary in great writing or great speaking:

(i) The first and most important is the power to conceive great thoughts...

(ii) The second is strong and inspired emotion *[pathos]*. (These two sources are for the most part natural; the remaining three involve art.)

(iii) Certain kinds of figures. (These may be divided into figures of thought and figures of speech.)

(iv) Noble diction. This has as subdivisions choice of words and the use of metaphorical and coined words.

(v) Finally, to round off the whole list, dignified and elevated word arrangement.[9]

According to this ancient writer, one may have a great idea *(logos)* and the ability to express it with passion *(pathos),* but the other three elements (a version of the Virtues of Style system) are what help the communicator to achieve excellence in the force of expression.

> Persuasion is on the whole something we can control, whereas amazement and wonder exert invincible power and force and get the better of every hearer. Experience in invention and ability to order and arrange material cannot be detected in single passages; we begin to appreciate them only when we see the whole context. Sublimity, on the other hand, produced at the right moment, tears everything up like a whirlwind, and exhibits the orator's power at a single blow.[10]

The simile "like a whirlwind" evocatively makes his point. It also speaks to every preacher's desire to capture the minds of listeners through an effective use of crafted language in the expression of the faith we passionately hold. Producing "the whirlwind" can only occur if the preacher has something profound to say and has the skill to say it profoundly.

PRODUCING "THE WHIRLWIND": STYLE AS WAY OF KNOWING AND WAY OF EXPRESSION

We have already covered this author's first two principles (*logos* and *pathos*) in previous chapters. The remaining three—effective control of the right word, effective control of the figures of thought and speech, and sensitive control of the lyric quality of language—are the essential resources of controlling the sermon's affective power in moving listeners. Our claim is that they are also essential resources that can help a preacher control the meaning that gets communicated in a sermon. Anyone who has ever struggled with wording an idea in just the right way, knows that sometimes, when you get it right, the words help you to express something more important or more exciting than you had in mind when you started. Control of these resources is about more than just connecting with the listeners in a powerful way. Control of these resources can even help a preacher figure out what it is that she or he wants to say by helping them discover new ways of thinking. Taking a closer look at each resource may help clarify what *we* mean.

Control of the "Right Word"

In the seventeenth century, the classical divisions between formal logic and rhetoric, or informal logic, were collapsed. Audience-centered argument theory and some aspects of arrangement were all gathered under the umbrella of a new field of dialectical logic. Rhetoric was reduced to little more than the study of style known as *elocution*. This was the art made famous by Professor Henry Higgins who sought to teach *My Fair Lady's* Eliza Doolittle how to sound like and act like a member of the educated class. It became an art intimately tied to class distinctions between Oxford trained aristocracy and commoners.

Even as it was shuttled to this ill-fated corner, style, as the study of improving one's ability in expression, continued to make a contribution to helping people learn to think in terms of how "what to say" will come across. This is because, learning how to speak *well* has always been an important aspect of rhetorical theory. Recall from chapter 2 that Quintilian even defined oratory as "a good man speaking well" (cf. 2.15). Control of one's language is still the mark of the one who would "speak well." You will get a sense of this if you read the following statement from Newman's *Idea of the University* aloud. We cited a portion of it in the epigraph of this chapter, but we think the whole statement on this subject is worth *hearing*. This is Newman the preacher as well as Newman the apologist for a truly liberal education speaking:

> Thought and speech are inseparable from each other. Matter and expression are parts of one: *style is a thinking out into language....* A great author, Gentlemen, is not one who merely has a *copia verborum*, whether in prose or verse, and can, as it were, turn on at his will any number of splendid phrases and swelling sentences; but he is one who has something to say and knows how to say it.... He writes passionately, because he feels keenly; forcibly, because he conceives vividly; he sees too clearly to be vague; he is too serious to be otiose; he can analyze his subject, and therefore he is rich; he embraces it as a whole and in its parts, and therefore he is consistent; he has a firm hold of it, and therefore he is luminous. When his imagination wells up, it overflows in ornament; when his heart is touched, it thrills along his verse. He always has the right word for the right idea, and never a word too much. If he is brief, it is because few words suffice; when he is lavish of them, still each word has its mark, and aids, not embarrasses, the vigorous march of his elocution.[11]

Did you notice in giving voice to the text how his comments become the embodiment of his argument. One can still hear Oxford-trained, albeit class and sexist, overtones in this statement much like the lessons of elocution made famous in *My Fair Lady.* However, like the author of *On the Sublime* before him, Newman is trying to describe the necessity of exercising a trained ability to express oneself with the genuine eloquence that should be the by-product of a truly liberal education.

Unlike the author of *On the Sublime*, Newman makes no distinction between form and content. Matter must be fitted to form and form to matter. Considered in this way word choice is not merely a vehicle of thought, nor some limited notion of mere ornamentation. It actually performs the author's persuasive intention, or quite literally, it functions as another "means of persuasion."[12] The idea that "style is thinking out into language" was a bold claim pressing the limits of the expressionist conception of style when Newman first gave it voice. Today, this is the governing assumption of most approaches to rhetorical uses of language.

We cannot separate arguments from the words we use to express them. The separation of rhetoric and dialectical logic completely ignored the contextual nature of arguments and language. Lucy teaches at an urban seminary. However, many of her students serve in small, rural churches on the eastern shore of Maryland. The members of their congregations have spent their lives fishing the waters of the Chesapeake Bay. Those students, who have previously only "met" crabs as disembodied sets of legs ready to be cracked and consumed in a restaurant or as crabcakes served by an adventurous cook, realize that they must quickly learn a new language in order to be heard. Finding the right word for the community, as we have noted in all of the other chapters, requires knowing the community and listening to the community. Only when you have listened to your brothers and sisters in Christ will you begin to understand how to "put it into their own words."

Control of "Figures of Thought and Figures of Speech"

Ancient rhetoricians were in love with tropes and figures. Much of what is called "the rhetorical handbook" tradition is filled with dictionary-like lists distinguishing everything from *accumulatio* (heaping up praise or accusation in a single sentence that emphasizes or summarizes points already made) to *zeugma* (a kind of ellipsis in which one verb governs several congruent words or clauses). Preachers who think such lists odd should note that, as a trained rhetorician, Newman would have been fully aware he was using *accumulatio* when he composed some of his sentences quoted in the previous section. Two essential resources to help preachers gain facility in using figures are Richard Lanham's *A Handlist of Rhetorical Terms* and the older massive study by Bullinger, *Figures of Speech Used in the Bible*.[13] The most useful aspect of both books is their inductive indexes which allow the reader who does not know the name of a figure to zero in on it by simply describing the movement or the effect. Once identified, both books provide good examples of the technique. They are marvelous tools to increase one's facility in the use of figures as a means of creating and controlling *force of expression*.

Force of expression is certainly a useful skill to develop, but others have begun to wonder about the use of figures as a resource in the *control of thought*. In the modern era many rhetoricians and philosophers have argued that at least four figures are actually master tropes humans use to render unfamiliar ideas by way of familiar ones. These tropes are metaphor, metonymy, synecdoche, and irony. They all work by a form of substitution based on either resemblance and difference, but the essential point is that they literally become ways speakers have to introduce listeners to new ways of knowing.[14] This means that there is a significant tensional relationship between the use of figures as "way of knowing" and "way of expression."

If there is space to discuss only one figure at any length it must be metaphor, and the most accessible introduction, without question, is Lakoff and Johnson's *Metaphors We Live By*. This book belongs on every pastor's desk. The authors make a very bold claim: metaphor is not just a matter of language as mere words. Rather, human thought process, itself, is largely metaphorical.[15] They examine how people structure meaning by such metaphors as "argument is war," "time is money," "love is a journey," and "problems are puzzles." Since the essence of metaphor is understanding and experiencing one kind of thing in terms of another, the authors invite readers to imagine what would happen to our way of knowing if we changed metaphors in significant cultural ideas. How might the U.S. culture be different today if, say, we had decided to collaborate, partnering with addicts in a *dance* to help them take steps to regain the *lead* in their life, rather than having declared *war*, making users the enemy to be housed in *prisoner-of-war* facilities? Lakoff and Johnson argue that metaphor can fundamentally order how we perceive reality because humans perceive what they view as reality through language filters.

Philosopher and theologian Paul Ricoeur, who has written extensively on the centrality and power of metaphor, argues that they are much more than mere substitutions or translations. "Real metaphors," he writes, "are not translatable."[16] These real metaphors must not be considered ornaments that make our speech elegant or engaging. Rather metaphors carry much of the weight of our knowledge and understanding. The depth of their meaning is inexhaustible, and they "offer new information... [telling] us something new about reality."[17]

The importance of understanding the evocative power of metaphor in preaching cannot be understated since it is the essential means by which a radical understanding of God and the life of faith are communicated in scripture: "All flesh is grass"; "The Lord is my Shepherd"; "God is my shield.... God is a righteous judge.... God will whet his sword; he has bent and strung his bow.... [against an enemy] pregnant with mischief"; "Whoever flatters a neighbor is spreading a net for the neighbor's feet"; "The Lord rises to argue his case; he stands to judge the peoples"; "a shoot shall come out of the stump of Jesse, and a branch shall grow out of his roots." Jesus' metaphors are equally rich: "You are the salt of the earth"; "The eye is the lamp of the body"; "Enter through the narrow gate"; "No one pours new wine in old wineskins"; "I am the light of the world"; "Give, and it will be given to you. A good measure, pressed down, shaken together, running over, will be put into your lap"; "This is my body"; "This cup that is poured out for you is the new covenant in my blood"; "The kingdom of God has come near."

One of the essential tasks of preaching, therefore, is the mastery of contemporary metaphor. We who preach are called upon to continue this revelatory task of discovering forceful and imaginative metaphors that reveal and embody the transformative power of gospel as bearers of a new reality. In *The Rule of Metaphor*, Ricoeur reminds us that "*Lively* expression is that which expresses existence as *alive*."[18] It is not enough to repeat and explain the old and, now, largely outdated or overused metaphors of scripture. When we encounter metaphor in scripture that embodies ways of knowing that were once radical expressions of knowing God and knowing the new realities of Christian life, the preacher's task is to find new ways to embody the freshness of the truth of such expressions in lively metaphors relevant to our context today. Anything less is less than preaching.

Control of the Lyric Quality of Language

Is "dignified and elevated word arrangement" the same thing as rhythm? Henry Mitchell notes that most "White observers" of Black preaching often stereotype Black style in terms of "rhythm in preaching." For his part, Mitchell says, after fifty years in the pulpit and much study of taped sermons by Black preachers he found little evidence of any rhythm or metrical beat. He agrees that there is certainly a Black style of intonation, a Black style of emphasis, and, on occasion, even musicality—but no specific Black cadence in preaching.[19] Of course, others trace many of the new venues of Black poetry and "rapping" through a tradition out of the Black sermon style that sought to bring a compelling effect of almost lyric quality to the control of word arrangement.[20] This kind of preaching works to bring about an experiential encounter with a goal of producing a climax of impression for the listener.[21] On occasion, it continues to resonate with the best lyric qualities of spacious eighteenth- and nineteenth-century American oratory. In the end, the question is not whether the affective use of schemes and tropes, the hallmark of a previous century's oratory, create an identifiable rhythm. The classical concept of rhythm never really entailed the idea of metrical beat or even musical intonation. Aristotle is often quoted in the literature at this point: "Prose should be rhythmical without becoming metrical." What it did entail has more to do with a fluid style of speech in which ideas get expressed with an ear for listening audiences rather than for readers. It had to do with the ability to create a pleasing flow of speech at one moment and speech filled with nobility in the next. We who live two millennia on the other side of the literate revolution find it difficult to listen to the reflections of an oral culture as it describes at length the importance of felicity in a certain smoothness of speaking style. Our frame of reference is almost wholly suited to listen for the logic of an idea rather than a sense of *satisfaction* in the way in which it gets expressed.

In this classical sense, Mitchell would probably find a good deal of Black preaching "rhythmical." In essence it is preaching shaped for the ear rather than prose shaped to be read. Complex syntactical constructions with subordinate clauses that may represent the best form of expression in a written essay are anathema in this kind of lyric presentation. On the other hand, parallelism and repetitions that build to a natural and anticipated climax are the height of this style.

When teaching public speaking, one of the points Bob tries to get across is the need for the student to put away the carefully manicured manuscript or the carefully structured, in-depth outline (the latter of which is always a course requirement) and talk to the audience. Artistic craft requires that the preacher work out the structure of a sermon in advance This entails control of the right word and control of the timely figure of speech that convey both ideas and the way they get expressed. Too often speakers stop at this point and end up orally delivering nothing more than a carefully composed literate essay. Even if such a composition is read with care to create listener contact, it will never sound like anything more than what it is—an essay. As a great orator once described it, this kind of presentation has "the smell of the lamp-wick about." The quality and conviction of a speech come only as the speaker is able to take up in himself or herself the well-practiced sense of what is to be said and then lets it be played out in a collaborative give and take with the listeners. This can still be achieved by using a brief, speaker's outline where key ideas serve as springboards to conversation with forethought. When expressed in this way, even complex ideas are forced to find clearer expression. In addition, the preacher who has manuscripted and then is able to put the manuscript aside, is perceived as one who trusts her or his convictions.

Oral rhythms can be dramatically effected by conscious, literate reflection and preparation. But to free these rhythms from the constraints of being a literate essay delivered orally, the speaker must find a way to let the "forethought" become conversation once again. When presented in this way, a natural almost contextual rhythm develops. This orally controlled event is at the heart of the natural, lyrical style in which preacher and people cocreate the sermon together.

THE DIMENSIONS OF STYLE IN REVIEW

In our efforts to give a relevant word of gospel in our time and in our place, most preachers do not see a necessity to produce sermons that will be forever regarded as sublime Christian *classics*. We suspect most preachers would count themselves faithful as long as they could produce a good "period piece," a sermon that captures something essential about our cultural moment and allows the gospel to speak to it with clarity of expression and compelling effect. But *clarity of expression* and *compelling effect* do not occur by accident. They are by-products of artistic control of the right word, artistic control of the figures of thought and speech, and artistic control of the lyric quality of language.

A contemporary rhetorician has suggested that *clarity of expression, compelling effect*, and *credible delivery* are the hallmarks of artistic control of style.[22] He distinguishes these dimensions of style from other qualities one might suggest because they correlate the concerns of style with the speaker's persuasive task. These are:

> The *Adaptive Dimension of Style* makes choices based on what is most effective in carrying meaning to an audience. For example, the speaker is applying the adaptive dimension of style whenever he or she chooses a synonym in place of a more

elaborate construction of words. This dimension correlates with *logos* as a means of persuasion and it translates the ancient principle of effective control of the right word into a contemporary concern.

The *Affective Dimension of Style* makes choices based on use of language that will appeal to the aesthetic tastes of the audience, engaging the emotions of listeners in less than obvious ways. For example, the speaker is applying the affective dimension of style whenever he or she chooses to use alliteration in order to achieve a sense of forcefulness in the expression of a series of ideas. This dimension of style correlates with *pathos* in the way it works on the emotions of the listeners and translates the ancient principle of control of the figures of thought and speech into a contemporary concern.

The *Ethical Dimension of Style* makes choices in the way language is conveyed that will enhance the speaker's image and the credible connection an individual makes with listeners. For example, the speaker is applying the ethical dimension of style whenever he or she moves away from the manuscript to speak from the heart. The correlation between *ethos* and this dimension is obvious and lends support to our translation of the ancient perception of sensitive control over the lyric quality of language.

We believe that these three dimensions represent the heart of what it means to adopt a balanced rhetorical stance concerning style in preaching. No one should assume that a balanced and sustained use will suddenly turn one into a pulpiteer. But on occasion, when used to express a terrific idea in which the speaker passionately believes, on that occasion, a skilled preacher may discover words coming together in a manner that "tear[s] everything up like a whirlwind."

FURTHERING THE CONVERSATION

Through effective and creative use of stylistic choices we make our sermons come alive. The vividness of the language we use and the images that we employ play an important part in helping us to connect with our listeners. We agree with John Killinger, "Style is the preacher's signature on the sermon."[23] Finding your own *voice* is part of discovering what a lyric quality of speaking looks and feels like for you. That makes it part of the *ethical dimension* of style, part of what makes sermonic composition and delivery a unique aspect of what, in chapter 3, we referred to as the *persona* one must develop as a preacher. But we have also presented a case to view style as something far more than finding one's idiosyncratic stamp in a sermon. In fact, style is often affected by many influences: by cultural norms and personal expectations, by confessional allegiances and liturgical necessities, by theological mentors and philosophic presuppositions. All of these are relevant elements in determining any one person's development of his or her own style. In this chapter, however, we have tried to address elements that are universal to the craft. Every preacher must embrace these aspects of style if she or he is at all concerned with "how it will come across."

On the Three Practices of Excellence

Rhetoricians down through the ages have encouraged students and practitioners alike to grasp that excellence is pursued through three practices:

- Through the study of the various precepts and principles of the art;

- Through continual practice and trained critique; and,

- By studying and imitating those who have mastered the art.

Of the three, practice and critique are the most helpful in turning technical knowledge into skilled artistic expression. Precepts and imitation can teach, but only critical practice lifts technical knowledge into versatility and excellence.

• QUESTION FOR GROUP DISCUSSION

Analyze either the text of (or a predefined portion of) a sermon which your group accepts as representative of the kind of excellence to be emulated in preaching. If possible use a text for which you have audiotape. Look and listen for instances of each of the three dimensions of style discussed in this chapter

or

Take an existing sermon of your own composition and analyze it according to the three dimensions of style. Revise the sermon with an ear to pushing what it can accomplish stylistically. Practice a lyric delivery. Then deliver the sermon before the discussion group and invite them to offer critique according to the three dimensions of style.

On Metaphor as Way of Knowing and Way of Expressing

Following Lakoff and Johnson and much of contemporary linguistic theory, we have suggested that metaphor and related tropes of understanding and experiencing one kind of thing in terms of another play a very significant part in structuring the way in which we derive "meaning" from reality. The New Testament is filled with this kind of forceful and imaginative language which functions as a gate through which Christians must pass if they are to realize their identity as members of a new community. In this sense Christian formation is largely a task of preaching these central metaphors and other tropical ways of knowing.

• QUESTION FOR GROUP DISCUSSION

In the gospels, Jesus speaks of the "Kingdom of God." Likewise, Paul also uses this figure of speech to describe God's reign and our place within the economy of God. Reflect upon the similarities and differences in the two uses of this metaphor.

A Final Thought: On the Issue of Control

Throughout this chapter we have explored the issue of style by discussing the ways that you, as the preacher, need to control what happens in the sermon. We have urged you to take control of the words you use, the images and figures of speech, as well as the lyric, oral character of the sermon. We have used the word *control* because we wish to impress upon you the fact that these are elements of the sermon that have strategic importance, and about which you must make choices. Style is not just frivolous ornamentation or something that happens "by accident." Style is as important as the arguments you make, the emotions you create, and the character you present. However, as we close this chapter, and the book, we need to qualify our use of control. Frequently, throughout the book, we have reminded you that when you are writing or delivering a sermon, you are in a relationship. You are in a relationship with God and you are in a relationship with your listeners. You cannot control what your listeners hear or think about what you are saying, anymore than they can control what you say. It is all a process of negotiation that grows out of a relationship of mutual love and respect set within the larger context of God's love and grace.

READ MORE ABOUT IT

George Lakoff and Mark Johnson. *Metaphors We Live By.* Chicago: University of Chicago Press, 1980.

Henry H. Mitchell. *Celebration & Experience in Preaching.* Nashville: Abingdon Press, 1990.

Robert C. Tannehill. *The Sword of His Mouth: Forceful and Imaginative Language in Synoptic Sayings.* Philadelphia/Missoula: Fortress Press and Scholars Press, 1975.

Chapter 8

The Art of Connecting

Nineteenth-century homiletics drew on rhetorical study. In the twentieth century, homiletic wisdom was reduced, while at the same time the connection between homiletics and rhetoric was severed. We decided to preach the Bible, to draw method from the Bible, and to turn away from the machinations of secular rhetoric. The result: We made biblical noises but in fact we did not preach very well. Of course, the black pulpit continued to speak with force, the force of a sophisticated black rhetorical tradition. But note, as theology moves toward philosophy and as biblical criticism connects with literary criticism, homiletics must shyly make up and relate to rhetoric once again.

—David Buttrick, *A Captive Voice*[1]

[David Buttrick's] genuine and lasting contribution is in the loud and long call he has issued to a church grown complacent about how it preaches. His call has amounted to a recovery of rhetoric. But it is more than that. It is a recovery of the awareness that we are shaped rhetorically willy-nilly. The question is not whether the church should utilize rhetoric in its preaching. The question is which rhetoric will the church use and toward what end.

—David M. Greenhaw, "The Formation of Consciousness"[2]

THE QUESTION IS, indeed, which rhetoric? It is not uncommon to see even the best of homileticians confuse the art of rhetoric with rationalism on one hand and literary studies on the other. We agree with David Buttrick and affirm David Greenhaw's perceptive analysis of Buttrick's greatest contribution. Our effort is clearly more modest than David Buttrick's *tour-de-force* proposal of a contemporary homiletic. In fact, we purposefully avoid advocating any one of the many contemporary methods of homiletic practice. Instead, we have written this work for homileticians and preachers who have decided that it is essential to "make up and relate to rhetoric once again." Our purpose has been to offer a basic *rhetoric* of preaching. Though a modest contribution to this most ancient of genres, we hope that by entering the conversation we have initiated, you have come to value, as we do, the necessity of adopting a rhetorical stance in preaching.

We began this book by encouraging readers to consider what it would mean to adopt a rhetorical stance in preaching. As Booth first presented it, a rhetorical stance in persuading an audience places the weight of balance equally on the three legs, *ethos*, *pathos*, and *logos*. To these three "legs" we have added contemporary conceptions of the significance of arrangement and style. We have argued that both of these facets of rhetoric also function as means of persuasion once we grasp the way in which they, like the three classical means of persuasion, *represent* "ways of knowing." So, in effect, our rhetoric offers a five-legged rather than a three-legged stool on which we call for balance. The point remains the same. What is required of a preacher who would adopt a rhetorical stance is to practice balance.

In his orginal address in which he proposed the necessity of teaching "The Rhetorical Stance," Booth was also commending that English teachers *make up and relate to rhetoric once again.* After he proposed this balanced "stance," he concluded by saying, "Now obviously the habit of seeking this balance is not the only thing we have to teach under the heading of rhetoric. But I think that everything worth teaching under that heading finds its justification finally in that balance."[3] We agree. We, Lucy and Bob, believe that a *balanced* conception of rhetoric is essential for the understanding of preaching as long as preaching is understood to be a humanistic task— a task of one human communicating with other humans concerning that which can be believed or can be affirmed among them.

In addition, when we take this concept of *balance* seriously it will keep us from falling into the trap of thinking that control of *logos* and invention, or *pathos* and passion, or *ethos* and persona, or *arrangement* and intention, or *style* and voice, will, like the equivalent of a mathematical formula, add up to great preaching. Control of any one of these without the balance adds up to a disaster. Balance in rhetoric is a synergy. Its whole is greater than the sum of its parts. Remember, rhetoric is an art, not a science. If you are making cranberry bread and you leave out the sugar, your family will give you funny looks when they bite into your trusted specialty. Cooking is a science. If you leave out a crucial ingredient, or mix the ingredients in the wrong way, your recipe will not work. Rhetoric, on the other hand is a way of knowing, a way of approaching and framing a task—that of speaking to persuade. While some of what we have said in this book may come across as rules, we think they are better understood as performance recommendations.

Recognizing this will mean two things for those of us who preach. One, we need to be willing to follow the "rules" but also to deviate from them when we feel that it is necessary. If, for example, you have come to know that your congregation responds well to something your preaching professor told you NEVER to do, as long as it is ethical, do it. Good artists are those who know the rules and, then, know how to break them. (What is important here is that you know the rules before you break them.) Remember, Picasso knew how to draw a human face, and he was good at it. But he wanted to experiment, and break the face into its geometric components. Cubism was born, out of investigation and experimentation, not ignorance and incompetence.

Second, understanding that rhetoric and preaching are arts should also alert us to the fact that they will be difficult and messy! There is no easy or standard recipe for a successful speech or sermon. An enlightening and challenging sermon comes only out of long hours of hard work. Those hours may feel frustrating, and there may be many times when you want to give up and turn to one of the many sermon services. But let us assure you. If you use someone else's sermon, your congregation will know because it will not have the freshness, the immediacy of a sermon that comes from your hard work.

When it feels as though you are getting nowhere, and you can't seem to make any progress, you need to realize that you are *not* failing; rather, you are truly engaging the text and the moment. Don't give up. Keep thinking, reflecting, praying. Work to maintain balance in your rhetorical stance. Then push through that plateau. The moment of insight and enlightenment will arrive and, because you have learned the art of balance, you will also have learned the art of connecting with your congregation.

Notes

All translations of Aristotle's *Rhetoric* are from George Kennedy, trans. and ed., *Aristotle on Rhetoric: A Theory of Civic Discourse: Newly Translated, with Introduction, Notes, and Appendices* (New York: Oxford University Press, 1991). Unless noted otherwise, all other translations of classical material are taken from the standard *Loeb* editions.

1. Who Needs Rhetoric?

1. From "The Drum Major Instinct," a sermon delivered February 4, 1968 at Ebenezer Baptist Church by Martin Luther King, Jr. In *I Have a Dream: Writings and Speeches that Changed the World*, James Melvin Washington, ed.; foreword by Coretta Scott King (San Francisco: Harper San Francisco, 1992), 191. The use of "them" and the shift to "him" is original to King.

2. Richard Lischer, *The Preacher KING: Martin Luther King, Jr. and the Word that Moved America* (Oxford: Oxford University Press, 1995), 12.

3. Karlyn Kohrs Campbell, *The Rhetorical Act*, 2nd ed. (Belmont, Calif.: Wadsworth Publishing, 1996), 8-9.

4. Ibid., 4.

5. Ibid., 8.

6. Ibid., 9.

7. Ibid.

8. Fred Craddock, "Is There Still Room for Rhetoric?" In *Preaching on the Brink: The Future of Homiletics*, Martha J. Simmons, ed. (Nashville: Abingdon Press, 1996), 68. We are aware that Craddock may have posed the question in this fashion by way of "indirection," but even though his final response is an unhesitating affirmation, we find that the way in which he posed the question still participates in the polarization of the disciplines.

9. Ibid., 72-73.

10. Richard Lischer, "Interview with Richard Lischer and William Willimon," interview by Steven Reagles, *Homiletic* 20, no. 2 (1995):15.

11. Ibid., 16.

12. Ibid.

13. Ibid., 20-21.

14. Campbell, *The Rhetorical Act*, 9.

15. See the remarks on the cadences of King's "Black English" in Henry Mitchell, *Black Preaching: The Recovery of a Powerful Art* (Nashville: Abingdon Press, 1990), 82.

16. Thomas G. Long, "And How Shall They Hear?" In *Listening to the Word:*

Studies in Honor of Fred B. Craddock, Gail R. O'Day and Thomas G. Long, eds. (Nashville: Abingdon Press, 1993), 178.

17. Campbell, *The Rhetorical Act,* 9.

18. Wayne C. Booth, "The Rhetorical Stance," in *College Composition and Communication* (October 1963); reprinted in *Landmark Essays on Rhetorical Invention in Writing,* Richard Young and Yameng Liu, eds. (Davis, Calif.: Hermagoras Press, 1994), 23-24.

19. Ibid., 26-27.

20. The content of this paragraph is largely appropriated from the review of David S. Cunningham, *Faithful Persausion: In Aid of a Rhetoric of Christian Theology* (Notre Dame: University of Notre Dame Press, 1991) by Robert S. Reid in the *Quarterly Journal of Speech* 79 (1993): 491-93.

21. Cunningham, *Faithful Persuasion,* xv.

22. Ibid., 27.

23. Cunningham acknowledges that others such as Elisabeth Schüssler Fiorenza and Rebecca Chopp have already advocated similar approaches in other areas of biblical study, 35. See Elisabeth Schüssler Fiorenza, "The Ethics of Interpretation: Decentering Biblical Scholarship," *Journal of Biblical Literature* 107, no. 1 (March 1988): 13-14; and Rebecca Chopp, "Theological Persuasion: Rhetoric, Warrants, and Suffering," in *Worldviews and Warrants: Plurality and Authority in Theology,* William Schweiker, ed. (Lanham, Md.: University Press of America, 1987), 18ff.

24. Wayne C. Booth, "Rhetoric and Religion: Are They Essentially Wedded?" in *Radical Pluralism and Truth: David Tracy and the Hermeneutics of Religion,* Werner G. Jeanrond and Jennifer L. Rilke, eds. (New York: Crossroad, 1991), 64.

25. Booth, "Rhetoric and Religion," 79. We suggest that students of homiletics who read Craddock's essay "Is There Still Room for Rhetoric?" would do well to read Booth's essay to hear the question raised in a wholly different key.

26. Martin Heidegger, "Letter on Humanism," in *Basic Writings,* David Farrell Krell, ed. (New York: Harper & Row: 1977), 217.

27. For example, see the essays in *The Rhetoric of the Human Sciences: Language and Argument in Scholarship and Public Affairs,* J. S. Nelson, A. Megill, and D. N. McCloskey, eds. (Madison: University of Wisconsin Press, 1987).

28. Herbert Simons, "The Rhetoric of Inquiry as an Intellectual Movement," *The Rhetorical Turn,* Herbert W. Simons, ed. (Chicago: University of Chicago Press, 1990), 21.

29. Long makes extensive use of the "marriage" metaphor to the point where he can describe Karl Barth as "unplugging the respirator" that finally severs the relationship (172-73). We would argue that Long merely describes the demise of a particular, historically located conception of the interrelatedness of rhetoric and homiletic. We agree that this paradigm has died.

30. For a highly readable yet very comprehensive introduction and contempo-

rary exploration of this genre the preacher can do no better that Edward P. J. Corbett's *Classical Rhetoric for the Modern Student*, 3rd ed. (New York: Oxford University Press, 1990).

31. John A. Broadus, *On the Preparation and Delivery of Sermons*, New and Revised Edition, ed. Jesse Burton Weatherspoon (New York: Harper & Brothers, 1944).

2. WHEN DID ALL THIS GET STARTED?

1. David James Randolph, *The Renewal of Preaching: A New Homiletic Based on the New Hermeneutic* (Philadelphia: Fortress Press, 1969), 21.

2. David Buttrick, *Homiletic: Moves and Structures* (Philadelphia: Fortress Press, 1989), 28.

3. Ibid., 41.

4. Randolph, *The Renewal of Preaching*, 54-55. For a generation that may already be unfamiliar with Perry Mason, he was a character in novels and in a television series. He was famous for revealing the actual crook or murderer during the trial and, against seemingly impossible odds, dramatically proving his own client innocence. The prosecution would frequently accuse Mason of "turning the courtroom into a circus."

5. Chaim Perelman and L. Olbrechts-Tyteca, *The New Rhetoric: A Treatise on Argumentation* (Notre Dame: University of Notre Dame Press, 1969), 190-92; and Chaim Perelman, *The Realm of Rhetoric* (Notre Dame: University of Notre Dame Press, 1982). See Buttrick, *Homiletic*, 40-42.

6. On Paul's rhetorical skill see David Aune, *The New Testament in Its Literary Environment*, The Library of Early Christianity, Wayne Meeks, ed. (Philadelphia: Westminster Press, 1987), 204-12 and George Kennedy, *New Testament Interpretation Through Rhetorical Criticism* (Chapel Hill: University of North Carolina Press, 1984).

7. On the audience-orientation of rhetoric see Aristotle, *Rhetoric*, 1.1.12. For the distinctions between logic, dialectic and rhetoric see Aristotle, *Topics* 1.1-3.

8. George Kennedy, trans. and ed., *Aristotle On Rhetoric: A Theory of Civic Discourse: Newly Translated, with Introduction, Notes, and Appendices* (New York: Oxford University Press, 1991), 37, n34.

9. Kennedy notes, "To *see* translates *theorêsai*, "to be an observer of and to grasp the meaning or utility of." English *theory* comes from the related noun *theoria*." Kennedy, trans. and ed., *Aristotle On Rhetoric*, 37, n34.

10. Wayne Booth, "The Rhetorical Stance." *Landmark Essays on Rhetorical Invention in Writing*, eds., R. E. Young and Y. Liu (Davis, Calif.: Hermagoras Press, 1994), 21.

11. Aristotle, *Rhetoric* 1.2.2-7.

12. Cicero *On Oratory* 2.27. For references to other ideas in this paragraph see *On Oratory* 2.130 and *Brutus* 185.

13. See Quintilian, *The Institutes* 2.15.

14. Ibid., 1.2.15.13.

15. Only with the advent of the twentieth century has the refined rhetoric, which until that time had always marked the speech of the educated elite, been replaced by the "middling English" of the modern discipline specific expert. See Kenneth Cmiel, *Democratic Eloquence: The Fight over Popular Speech in Nineteenth-Century America* (New York: William Morrow, 1990), 262.

16. C. S. Lewis, *European Literature in the Sixteenth Century* (Oxford: Clarendon Press, 1954), 61.

17. See Aune, *The New Testament in Its Literary Environment*, 202.

18. See James J. Murphy, "St. Augustine and the Debate About a Christian Rhetoric," *Quarterly Journal of Speech* 46 (1960), 400-10.

19. James J. Murphy in *Rhetoric in the Middle Ages: A History of Rhetorical Theory from St. Augustine to the Renaissance* (Berkeley: University of California Press, 1974), 53.

20. Ibid., 55.

21. Augustine, *On Christian Doctrine* 2.36.

22. Ibid., 2.40 and 4.17.

23. See Guibert de Nogent, "A Book About the Way a Sermon Ought to Be Given," trans. Joseph M. Miller, in *Readings in Medieval Rhetoric*, eds. Joseph M. Miller, Michael H. Prosser, and Thomas W. Benson (Bloomington, Ind.: Indiana University Press, 1973), 170-71. See Harry Caplan, "The Four Senses of Scriptural Interpretation and the Medieval Theory of Preaching," *Speculum* 4 (1929): 282-90. Nicholas of Lyra developed a poetic ditty to assist students in memorizing the distinctions, "Litera gesta docet, quid credas allegoria, Moralis quid agas, quo tendas anagogia." Which is to say,

> The *literal* sense teaches what actually happened,
> The *allegorical* what you are to believe,
> The *moral* how you are to behave,
> The *anagogical* where you are going.

Cited in F. F. Bruce, "The History of New Testament Study," *New Testament Interpretation: Essays on Principles and Methods*, ed. I. Howard Marshall (Grand Rapids, Mich.: Eerdmans, 1977), 28.

24. Robert of Basevorn, *The Form of Preaching*, Leopold Krul, O.S.B., Trans., in James J. Murphy, ed., *Three Medieval Rhetorical Arts* (Berkeley: University of California Press, 1971), 138.

25. Thomas Aquinas, *Summa Theologica*, Book I, Question I, Article 10, Reply to Objection 1. See Harry Caplan, "A Late Medieval Tractate on Preaching," *Studies in Rhetoric and Public Speaking in Honor of James Albert Winans*,

A. M. Drummond, ed. (New York: Russell & Russell Co., 1962), 67-68.

26. Michael Halloran, "Rhetoric in the American College Curriculum," *Pre/Text: The First Decade* (Pittsburgh: University of Pittsburgh Press, 1993), 96.

27. Ronald F. Reid, "Disputes over Preaching Method, the Second Awakening and Ebenezer Porter's Teaching of Sacred Rhetoric," *The Journal of Communication and Religion* 18 (1995): 6.

28. Phillips Brooks, *Lectures on Preaching: The Yale Lectures on Preaching, 1877* (Grand Rapids, Mich.: Baker Book House, 1969), 160-61.

29. Patricia Bizzell and Bruce Herzberg, "Enlightenment Rhetoric," *The Rhetorical Tradition: Readings From Classical Times to the Present*, Bizzell and Herzberg, eds. (Boston: St. Martin's Press, 1990), 657.

30. See Walter Jost, *Rhetorical Thought in John Henry Newman* (Columbia: University of South Carolina Press, 1989), 8.

31. John Henry Newman, *An Essay in Aid of a Grammar of Assent* (Notre Dame: University of Notre Dame, 1979), 90.

32. Ibid., 89.

33. Ibid., 282.

34. In the introduction to the re-issue of Newman's study Christopher Lash notes, "In an intellectual climate in which post-Enlightenment rationalism is presumed to be normative for the exercise of human rationality, Newman's lifelong hostility to rationalism is bound to be 'misunderstood.' In such a climate, emphasis on 'the personal conquest of truth' is invariably misconstrued as 'subjectivism.' It is therefore not surprising that, from the Modernist crisis to our own day, Newman has frequently been charged with 'irrationalism,' 'fideism,' and cognate vices"; Lash, "Introduction" in *Grammar*, 8. Aside from Vatican 2's reaffirmation, we think David Cunningham's *Faithful Persuasion: In Aid of a Rhetoric of Christian Theology* (Notre Dame: University of Notre Dame Press, 1991) is a modern reappropriation of Newman's task for a new generation of theologians.

35. John A. Broadus, "Author's Preface to the First Edition," *On the Preparation and Delivery of Sermons*, New and Revised Edition, ed. Jesse Burton Weatherspoon (New York: Harper & Brothers, 1944), xii. Unusual capitalization is original.

36. See James L. Golden and Edward P. J. Corbett, eds., *The Rhetoric of Blair, Campbell, and Whately* (Carbondale: Southern Illinois University Press, 1990).

37. David Buttrick, *A Captive Voice: The Liberation of Preaching* (Louisville, Ky.: Westminster/John Knox Press, 1994), 71.

38. Randolph, *The Renewal of Preaching*, vii.

39. For an intial survey effort See Richard L. Eslinger, *A New Hearing: Living Options in Homiletical Method* (Nashville: Abingdon Press, 1987), 13-14. For a more recent effort see Lucy Rose, *Sharing the Word: Preaching in the Roundtable Church* (Louisville: Westminister/John Knox, 1997).

40. Robert S. Reid, Jeffrey Bullock, and David Fleer, "Preaching as the Creation of an Experience: The Not-So-Rational Revolution of the New Homiletic," *The Journal of Communication and Religion* 18 (1995): 1-9.

41. We discuss the relationship of emphases and approaches to preaching at greater length in chapter 6.

42. In his *Philosophy of Rhetoric*, I. A. Richards had already suggested that rhetoric had reached its nadir with Whately (1936; rpt. New York: Oxford University Press, 1965), 5. Aside from Richards, Perelman's and Olbrechts-Tyteca's *The New Rhetoric* and Kenneth Burke's various *Rhetoric of Motives* were already challenging the reduction of rhetoric to a kind of logic. At about the same time as the New Homiletic(s) began to emerge, other rhetoricians were transforming the discipline. Edward P. J. Corbett had just published *Classical Rhetoric for the Modern Student* in 1965 (3rd ed., Oxford: Oxford University Press, 1990), Richard McKeon's essays on "Invention" and "Discovery" were being published during this period (collected in *Rhetoric: Essays in Invention and Discovery*, Mark Backman, ed. [Woodbridge, Conn.: Ox Bow Press, 1987]) and Edwin Black's seminal work, *Rhetorical Criticism: A Study in Method* (Madison: University of Wisconsin Press, 1965) was giving birth to a new generation of rhetorical critics.

43. For example, see the essays in John S. Nelson, Allan Megill, and Donald McCloskey, eds., *The Rhetoric of the Human Sciences: Language and Argument in Scholarship and Public Affairs* (Madison: University of Wisconsin Press, 1987). The present volume is also an example of "a rhetoric"; in this instance, a "rhetoric of preaching."

3. WHO DO THEY THINK I AM?

1. James M. Kouzes and Barry Z. Posner, *The Leadership Challenge: How to Keep Getting Extraordinary Things Done in Organizations* (San Francisco: Jossey-Bass, 1995), 31.

2. Aristotle, *Rhetoric* 2.1.5.

3. Ibid., 1.2.4.

4. See Quintilian, *The Institutes*, 2.15.

5. Alisdair MacIntyre writes, "An Aristotelian theory of the virtues does therefore presuppose a crucial distinction between what any particular individual at any particular time takes to be good for him and what is really good for him as a man. It is for the sake of achieving the latter good that we practice the virtues and we do so by making choices about means to achieve that end.... [It] is worth remembering Aristotle's insistence that the virtues find their place not just in the life of the individual, but in the life of the city and that the individual is indeed intelligible only as a *politikon zôon*." Alisdair MacIntyre, *After Virtue*, 2nd. ed. (Notre Dame: University of Notre Dame Press, 1984), 150.

6. Phillips Brooks, *Lectures on Preaching: The Yale Lectures on Preaching, 1877* (Grand Rapids: Baker Book House, 1978), 5.

7. Susan K. Hedahl, "Character," *Concise Encyclopedia of Preaching*, William H. Willimon and Richard Lischer, eds. (Louisville: Westminster John Knox Press, 1995), 67.

8. This paragraph uses the language of leadership theory from Kouzes and Posner's *The Leadership Challenge*. Most of contemporary leadership theory is a theory of influence—influencing the *want to* of followers—and, as such, it is rooted in rhetoric through and through. The assumption that leaders are to uphold virtues common to the community is not *just* a religious argument. It is a rhetorical argument.

9. Fred B. Craddock, *Preaching* (Nashville: Abingdon Press, 1985), 69.

10. Flannery O'Connor, "Revelation," in *The Complete Stories of Flannery O'Connor* (New York: Farrar, Straus, & Giroux, 1971).

11. This discussion of subtext is indebted to Fred Craddock.

12. Aristotle, *Rhetoric,* 1.2.2.

13. For a fuller discussion of Aristotle's understanding of the various types of proofs, we would suggest turning to George Kennedy's excellent textbook on rhetoric. George Kennedy, *Classical Rhetoric and Its Christian and Secular Tradition From Ancient to Modern Times* (Chapel Hill: University of North Carolina Press, 1980), 68-70, and Kennedy's more recent synthesis *A New History of Classical Rhetoric* (Princeton: Princeton University Press, 1994), 56-60.

14. Thomas G. Long, *The Witness of Preaching* (Louisville: Westminster/John Knox Press, 1989), 23-41.

15. Roderick P. Hart, *Modern Rhetorical Criticism* (Glenview, Ill.: Scott, Foresman/Little, Brown Higher Education, 1990), 251.

16. Ibid., 278-83.

17. Ibid., 292-93.

18. Bernard J. F. Lonergan, "Dialectic of Authority," in *A Third Collection: Papers by Bernard J. F. Lonergan, S. J.,* ed. Frederick E. Crowe (New York: Paulist Press, 1985), 5-12.

19. Charles Bartow and Richard Ward have done much to widen our understanding of the importance of delivery to the preaching project and especially to its function in the creation of *ethos*. See Charles Bartow, *The Preaching Moment: A Guide to Sermon Delivery* (Nashville: Abingdon Press, 1981); Charles Bartow *Effective Speech Communication in Leading Worship* (Nashville: Abingdon Press, 1988); and Richard F. Ward, *Speaking from the Heart: Preaching with Passion* (Nashville: Abingdon Press, 1992).

20. David Buttrick, *Moves and Structures* (Philadelphia: Fortress, 1987), 142.

21. See Long, *The Witness of Preaching,* 177-78; Richard L.Thulin, *The "I" of the Sermon* (Minneapolis: Fortress, 1989); and J. Randall Nichols, *The Restoring Word: Preaching as Pastoral Communication* (San Francisco: Harper and Row, 1987), 111-15.

22. Hart, *Modern Rhetorical Criticism*, 276.

23. Ibid., 277.

4. HOW WILL THEY COME TO CARE?

1. James Berkley, ed., *Preaching to Convince* (Waco, Tex.: Word Books, 1986), 53.

2. Citations from the "Pastoral Letter," *American Rhetorical Discourse*, 2nd ed., Ronald F. Reid, ed. (Prospect Heights: Waveland Press, 1995), 363-67. For Sarah Grimké's response see "A Letter Written in Response to the Pastoral Letter," 368-72.

3. Aristotle, *Rhetoric* 1.2.3.

4. According to George Kennedy, Book 2, chapters 2–11 of Aristotle's *Rhetoric* is "the earliest systematic discussion of human psychology" discussed as a means of "disposing" listeners to be persuaded by the speaker. George Kennedy, trans. and ed., *Aristotle On Rhetoric: A Theory of Civic Discourse: Newly Translated, with Introduction, Notes, and Appendices* (New York: Oxford University Press, 1991), 122-24.

5. L. A. Kosman, "Being Properly Affected: Virtues and Feelings in Aristotle's Ethics," *Essays on Aristotle's Ethics*, Amélie Oksenberg Rorty, ed. (Berkeley: University of California Press, 1980), 104-5.

6. Eugene Garver, *Aristotle's Rhetoric: An Art of Character* (Chicago: University of Chicago Press, 1994), 116.

7. Ibid., 111.

8. Kenneth Burke, *A Rhetoric of Motives* (Berkeley: University of California Press, 1950), 81.

9. A story of Meng-Tseu (at 1.7 in Pauthier, *Confucius et Mencius* [Paris: Charpentier, 1852], 230) cited by Chaim Perelman and L. Olbrects-Tyteca, *The New Rhetoric: A Treatise on Argumentation*, John Wilkinson and Purcell Weaver, trans. (Notre Dame: University of Notre Dame Press, 1969), 116.

10. Chaim Perelman, *The Realm of Rhetoric* (Notre Dame: University of Notre Dame Press, 1982), 35.

11. "Interview with Richard Lischer and William Willimon," interview by Steven Reagles in *Homiletic* 2 (1995): 16; and Craig A. Loscalzo, *Preaching Sermons That Connect* (Downers Grove, Ill.: InterVarsity Press, 1992).

12. Burke, *A Rhetoric of Motives*, 19-46. For this summary of Burke's distinctions in creating identification see Sonja K. Foss, Karen A. Trapp, and Robert Trapp, *Contemporary Perspectives on Rhetoric* (Prospect Heights: Waveland Press, 1985), 158-59.

13. David Buttrick, *Homiletic: Moves and Structures* (Philadelphia: Fortress Press, 1987), 33; for the intentions of a basic Christian rhetoric, see 41-42.

14. Ibid., 42.

15. Douglas Park, "The Meanings of 'Audience,'" *Landmark Essays on Rhetorical Invention in Writing*, Richard Young and Yameng Liu, eds. (Davis, Calif.: Hermagoras Press, 1994), 185-86. Original essay in *College English* (March 1982).

16. Walter Ong, "The Writer's Audience Is Always a Fiction," *Studies in the Evolution of Consciousness and Culture* (Ithaca, N.Y.: Cornell University Press, 1977), 73-74.

17. The classic presentation of this approach to audience is found in Lloyd Bitzer, "The Rhetorical Situation," *Philosophy and Rhetoric* 1 (1968): 1-12.

18. Richard Weaver, "The Spaciousness of Old Rhetoric," *The Ethics of Rhetoric* (Davis, Calif.: Hermagoras Press, 1985), 164-85.

19. Bob owns a turn of the century copy of *The Expositors Dictionary of Texts* published by Hodder and Stoughton in 1910. This massive two volume set has over two thousand pages of sermons by various preachers on most chapters of the Bible from Genesis through Revelation.

20. Leonora Tubbs Tisdale, *Preaching as Local Theology and Folk Art* (Minneapolis: Fortress Press, 1997).

21. On empathetic and dialogic listening skills see John Stewart and Carol Logan, *Together: Communicating Interpersonally*, 5th ed. (Boston: McGraw-Hill, 1998), 185-208. Stewart and Logan's text is theologically friendly because of the way in which it develops much of its insights from the Jewish theologian Martin Buber. For an important model of preaching that explores the idea of "listening as a collaborative conversation" in greater depth see John S. McClure, *The Roundtable Pulpit: Where Leadership & Preaching Meet* (Nashville: Abingdon Press, 1995).

22. Buttrick, *Homiletic*, 77.

5. WHAT AM I GOING TO SAY?

1. Zahava Karl McKeon, *Novels and Arguments: Inventing Rhetorical Criticism* (Chicago: University of Chicago Press, 1982), 24.

2. David Cunningham, *Faithful Persuasion: In Aid of a Rhetoric of Christian Theology* (Notre Dame: University of Notre Dame Press, 1990), 148-49.

3. We are using the name of Machiavellian in the popular sense of exercising a mastery of language in a manner characterized by expediency, deceit, and cunning. However, as rhetoricians we are also aware that this is an unfortunate malapropism when it comes to the true art of rhetoric Machiavellian taught *The Prince*. See Eugene Garver, *Machiavelli and the History of Prudence* (Madison: University of Wisconsin Press, 1987).

4. Examples include, Richard Lischer, "Preaching as the Church's Language," *Listening to the Word: Studies in Honor of Fred B. Craddock*, eds. Gail R. O'Day and Thomas G. Long (Nashville: Abingdon Press, 1997), 113-30 and

Lucy Rose, *Sharing the Word: Preaching in the Roundtable Church* (Louisville: Westminster/John Knox Press, 1997). For a discussion of this see Lucy Lind Hogan, "Rethinking Persuasion" in the 1997 Papers of the Annual Meeting of the Academy of Homiletics, 143-52.

5. If you are interested in more fully exploring how rhetoric works as argument, we suggest you begin with the writings of Kenneth Burke, in particular his book *A Rhetoric of Motives* (Berkeley: University of California Press, 1969); or Chaim Perelman and Lucie Olbrechts-Tyteca, *The New Rhetoric*, trans. John Wilkinson and Purcell Weaver (Notre Dame: University of Notre Dame Press, 1969). McKeon updates argument theory for the last quarter of the twentieth century in *Novels and Arguments: Inventing Rhetorical Criticism* (Chicago: University of Chicago Press, 1982). A recent introduction to discovering how arguments get used in different ways in academic disciplines and in the public sphere is found in the important collection of essays in Nelson, Megill, and McCloskey, *The Rhetoric of Human Sciences: Language and Argument in Scholarship and Public Affairs* (Madison: University of Wisconsin Press, 1987) and in George L. Dillon, *Contending Rhetorics: Writing in Academic Disciplines* (Bloomington: Indiana University Press, 1991).

6. *Rhetoric* 1.2.19.

7. Stephen Toulmin, *The Uses of Argument* (Cambridge: Cambridge University Press, 1958), 97-100.

8. Bruce Rosenberg, *Can These Bones Live: The Art of the American Folk Preacher,* revised edition (Urbana: University of Illinois Press, 1988), 8.

9. This is a paraphrase of the appropriate response John Claypool arrives at in a book of sermons surrounding the diagnosis and then death of his daughter from leukemia. A month after his daughter died Claypool preached a sermon in which he said, "I am here to testify that this is the only way down from the Mountain of Loss. I do not mean to say that such a perspective makes things easy, for it does not. But at least it makes things bearable when I remember that Laura Lue was a gift, pure and simple, something I neither earned nor deserved nor had a right to. And when I remember that the appropriate response to a gift, even when it is taken away, is gratitude, then I am better able to try and thank God that I was ever given her in the first place." John Claypool, *Tracks of a Fellow Struggler: How to Handle Grief* (Waco: Word Books, 1974), 82.

10. Rose, *Sharing the Word*, 90.

11. Ibid., 97.

12. Ibid., 133.

13. David Buttrick, *A Captive Voice: The Liberation of Preaching* (Louisville: Westminister / John Knox Press), 48.

14. Toulmin, *The Uses of Argument*, 99.

15. Ibid., 104.

6. WHAT DO I HOPE WILL HAPPEN?

1. Ben Shahn, *The Shape of Content* (Cambridge: Harvard University Press, 1957), 53.

2. Thomas Troeger, *Imagining a Sermon* (Nashville: Abingdon Press, 1990), 39-47.

3. George Kennedy, trans. and ed., *Aristotle On Rhetoric: A Theory of Civic Discourse: Newly Translated, with Introduction, Notes, and Appendices* (New York: Oxford University Press, 1991), 258.

4. Quintilian 7.10.13.

5. Karlyn Kohrs Campbell, *The Rhetorical Act*, 2nd ed. (Belmont, Calif.: Wadsworth Publishing, 1996), 243.

6. A recent exception to this is Ronald J. Allen, ed. *Patterns of Preaching: A Sermon Sampler* (St. Louis: Chalice Press, 1998). This book offers a very clear set of distinctions in patterns and purposes in preaching.

7. The discussion of the four paradigms of preaching presented in this section are adapted from Robert S. Reid, "Faithful Preaching: Preaching Epistemes, Faith Stages and Rhetorical Practice," in press with *Journal of Communication and Religion* (Nov. 1998).

8. Whatever crisis the biblical theology movement may have experienced in academia, it has dramatically shaped this approach which assumes that each text must be interpreted in light of its own historical context and in light of progressive revelation before it can be proclaimed as an authoritative word for contemporary congregations. It is this movement that largely gave rise to the search for the essential *kerygma*. Mounce declares of this approach, "The real answer to the question of the relevancy of the *kerygma* is found in the new understanding of the essential nature of preaching. If preaching be the extension in time of God's redemptive act, then not only may we preach the kerygma today, but we must. Nothing else is truly relevant.... The *kerygma* is the unique and divinely ordained medium for conveying the saving activity of God." Robert Mounce, *The Essential Nature of New Testament Preaching* (Grand Rapids: Eerdmans, 1960), 156.

9. Shared during a presentation on preaching for preachers by Lloyd Ogilvie, The Whitworth Institute, Spokane, Wash., July, 1990.

10. The speech pattern, developed by Allan Monroe in the 1930s, can be found in any standard public speaking text.

11. Henry Mitchell, *Black Preaching: The Recovery of a Powerful Art* (Nashville: Abingdon Press, 1990), 114.

12. Shared during a convocation on preaching by Paul Wilson at Wesley Theological Seminary, Wash., D.C., April, 1997 and discussed in detail in *The Four Pages of the Sermon: A Complete Guide to Biblical Preaching* (forthcoming from Abingdon Press). In surveying the possibilities of arrangement theory in *The Practice of Preaching* (Nashville, Abingdon Press 1995), 199, Wilson

states that, "[O]ur controlling purpose throughout is reflected in James S. Stewart's theological test of a sermon for a congregation: 'Did they, or did they not, meet God, today?' "

13. See Richard Eslinger, *A New Hearing: Living Options in Homiletic Method* (Nashville: Abingdon Press, 1987); Paul S. Wilson, *Imagination of the Heart: New Understandings in Preaching* (Nashville: Abingdon Press, 1988), 22-23.

14. This is the language of Hans Georg Gadamer and Paul Ricoeur. For example, on Ricoeur's use of the term "second *naïveté*" see Lewis S. Mudge, "Introduction: Paul Ricoeur on Biblical Interpretation," *Essays on Biblical Interpretation* by Paul Ricoeur. Lewis Mudge, ed. (Philadelphia: Fortress Press, 1980), 23.

15. Ricoeur, *Time and Narrative*, vol. 3 (Chicago: University of Chicago Press, 1988), 175.

16. John McClure, *The Roundtable Pulpit: Where Leadership and Preaching Meet* (Nashville: Abingdon Press, 1995), 45.

17. Eugene Lowry, *The Homiletical Plot* (Atlanta: John Knox Press, 1980).

18. David Buttrick, *Homiletic: Moves and Structures* (Fortress Press, Philadelphia, 1987), 28.

19. In later writings, Craddock moved away from the term "inductive preaching" and its association with logical argument structures, adopting the notion of "indirection" (from Kierkegaard) in which a sermon's "*nod* of recognition" becomes the "*shock* of recognition." Craddock states, "Without the nod, that is the sense of already knowing and agreeing, the shock of recognition, that is, the sudden realization that I am the one called, the one addressed, the one guilty, the one responsible, the one commissioned, is not even possible." Fred Craddock, *Preaching* (Nashville: Abingdon Press, 1985), 160.

20. For example, Campbell rejects Craddock's inductive approach as still subordinating Christ to a liberal theology of human experience and rejects the story and narrative approaches of the New Homiletic as still giving the story of the world priority over the storied identity of Christ in scripture. Hans Frei, the postliberal theorist upon whom Campbell formulates his homiletic, called for a "non-referential" exegetical practice in which the meaning of biblical texts remains internal to the logic and language of the texts themselves. In other words, texts do not refer to *heilsgeschichte*, or any experience of God, or God's saving acts external to the text. Texts only refer to the world they construe (Campbell, 12-16). In many ways, Thoroughly Postmodern approaches to preaching are like Traditional approaches in the way they resist letting experience externalize truth. However, postliberal conceptions of discursive truth are radically different from the Traditional approach's acceptance of truth as an externally revealed reality. Charles Campbell, *Preaching Jesus: New Directions for Homiletics in Hans Frei's Postliberal Theology* (Grand Rapids: Eerdmans 1997).

21. For Lischer's fully developed advocacy of a Postliberal preaching see Richard Lischer, "Preaching as the Church's Language," *Listening to the Word: Studies*

in Honor of Fred B. Craddock, Gail R. O'Day and Thomas G. Long, eds. (Nashville: Abingdon Press, 1997), 113-30; cite at 126.

22. Ibid., 128-29.

23. Richard Lischer, *A Theology of Preaching: The Dynamics of the Gospel* (Nashville: Abingdon, 1981), 48-50.

24. Ibid., 49.

25. Campbell, *Preaching Jesus*, 219.

26. Ibid., 231-41.

27. Craddock, *Preaching*, 172-74. The fourfold functions of form are from Craddock.

28. R. E. O. White, *A Guide to Preaching: A Practical Primer in Homiletics* (Grand Rapids: Eerdmans, 1973), 26.

29. Richard Eslinger, *Narrative and Imagination: Preaching the Worlds that Shape Us* (Minneapolis: Augsburg Fortress, 1995), 35.

7. How Will It Come Across?

1. John Henry Newman, *The Idea of a University* (Notre Dame: University of Notre Dame Press, 1878, 1982), 208, 219-20. Italics ours for the phrase *"style is a thinking out into language."*

2. Donald Macleod, *The Problem of Preaching* (Philadelphia: Fortress, 1987), 12-13.

3. On this see Robert Wuthnow, *The Restructuring of American Religion: Society and Faith Since World War II* (Princeton: Princeton University Press, 1988). Wuthnow sees this decentering as occurring in proportion to the increase of locating the quest for spirituality in the small group experience; see Wuthnow, *Sharing the Journey: Support Groups and America's New Quest for Community* (New York: The Free Press, 1994).

4. Richard Weaver, "The Spaciousness of Old Rhetoric," *The Ethics of Rhetoric* (Regnery/Gateway, 1953), reprint (Davis, Calif.: Hermagoras Press, 1985), 164-85.

5. Cicero, *Orator* 101.

6. A number of rhetoricians devoted whole books to the subject like Demetrius's *On Style* (ca. 2nd century B.C.), Dionysius *On the Arrangement of Words* (ca. 1st century B.C.), and Hermogenes's *On Types of Style* (ca. 2nd century A.D.).

7. Leonora M. Tubbs Tisdale, "The Calling of the Preacher," *Best Advice for Preaching*, John S. McClure, ed. (Minneapolis: Fortress, 1998), 8.

8. Aristotle, *Rhetoric*, 3.2-5.

9. D. A. Russell's translation of *On the Sublime* 8.1; parenthetical remarks are original to the author; bracketed words are ours. Also, in the fourth source of

great writing Russell actually concludes the sentence with "... of metaphorical and artificial language" and offers a footnote to indicate that "artificial" should be understood to mean "coined words." We simply have provided the clarification in the text and noted the change here; D. A. Russell and M. Winterbottom, *Ancient Literary Criticism: The Principle Texts in New Translations* (New York: Oxford University Press, 1972), 467.

10. Ibid., 1.4.

11. John Henry Newman, *The Idea of a University* (Notre Dame: University of Notre Dame Press, 1878, 1982), 208, 219-20. Italics are ours for the phrase *"style is a thinking out into language."*

12. Edward P. J. Corbett, *Classical Rhetoric for the Modern Student*, 3rd ed. (New York: Oxford University Press, 1990), 381.

13. Richard A. Lanham, *A Handlist of Rhetorical Terms*, 2nd ed. (Berkeley: University of California Press, 1991) and E. W. Bullinger, *Figures of Speech Used in the Bible* (Grand Rapids: Baker, 1978). Corbett also has an extensive list of schemes and tropes but no inductive indexes; *Classical Rhetoric*, 424-60.

14. For an extended discussion of the value and problems with the Four Master Tropes concept see Brian Vickers, *In Defense of Rhetoric* (Oxford: Clarendon Press, 1988), 435-79.

15. George Lakoff and Mark Johnson, *Metaphors We Live By* (Chicago: University of Chicago Press, 1980), 6.

16. Paul Ricoeur, *Interpretation Theory: Discourse and the Surplus of Meaning* (Fort Worth, Tex.: Texas Christian University Press, 1976), 52.

17. Ricoeur, *Interpretation*, 53.

18. Paul Ricoeur, *The Rule of Metaphor: Multi-disciplinary Studies of the Creation of Meaning in Language* (Toronto: University of Toronto Press, 1977), 43.

19. Henry Mitchell, *Black Preaching: The Recovery of a Powerful Art* (Nashville: Abingdon, 1990), 91-2.

20. On "rap" see Frederick W. Norris, "The Catholicity of Black Preaching" *Sharing Heaven's Music: The Heart of Christian Preaching—Essays in Honor of James Earl Massey*, Barry L. Callen, ed. (Nashville: Abingdon, 1995), 141.

21. On Massey's sense that Black preaching builds to a "climax of impression" see Cheryl J. Sanders, "God's Trombones: Voices in African American Folk Preaching," *Sharing Heaven's Music*, 160.

22. Richard P. Fulkerson, "The Public Letter as a Rhetorical Form: Structure, Logic, and Style in King's 'Letter from Birmingham Jail,' *Quarterly Journal of Speech* 65 (1979): 130. Reprinted in Corbett, *Classical Rhetoric*, 533.

23. John Killinger, *Fundamentals of Preaching* (Philadelphia: Fortress Press, 1985), 133.

8. THE ART OF CONNECTING

1. David Buttrick, *A Captive Voice: The Liberation of Preaching* (Loiusville: Westminster / John Knox, 1994), 3.

2. David M. Greenhaw, "The Formation of Consciousness," *Preaching as a Theological Task: World, Gospel, Scripture: Essays in Honor of David Buttrick*, Thomas G. Long and Edward Farley, eds. (Louisville: Westminster / John Knox, 1996), 13.

3. Wayne C. Booth, "The Rhetorical Stance," *College Composition and Communication* (October 1963); reprinted in *Landmark Essays on Rhetorical Invention in Writing*, Richard Young and Yameng Liu, eds. (Davis, Calif.: Hermagoras Press, 1994), 28.